I first met Neal in Nigeria in the early �__ ___
his parents Ron and Jerry Childs in Benin City and working with
Archbishop Benson Idahosa's ministry. Growing up in Africa
gave Neal a fresh new approach to life as he had to learn how
to make do in very harsh conditions. It prepared him for his
present-day ministry in Niger. Neal's new book, **BEYOND ONE**,
is more than just his story. It's a new generational approach
to leadership and ministry that is not only working in Africa,
but when implemented properly can work anywhere in the
world. It has been an honor to partner with him and his dear
wife Danette for many years now. I heartily endorse Neal's
ministry. I believe that when you read this book you will be
greatly blessed.

Richard Roberts
Oral Roberts Evangelistic Association, President

In his opening remarks, Neal Childs shares a key point in fully
understanding the calling of a true apostle - fulfilling the Great
Commission requires both a missional approach and a
generational approach to ministry. The heart of Jesus'
teaching to His disciples was generational. Without this
revelation, the Great Commission cannot be accomplished.

Oral Roberts was told by God to take healing to his generation,
but he also taught his students to reach their generation, and
that their work should exceed his.

Neal, Danette, and their children, both biological and spiritual,
carry this revelation into the next generation. Their
understanding, their love for people, and experience is
contagious. So, as you read this book, get ready for a new
energy and a new anointing.

Pastor Happy Caldwell
Agape Church, Pastor Emeritus
Victory Television Network, Founder & President

BEYOND ONE presents the challenge of our generation. The pages of this book are a clarion call, solidly based in scripture and presented with incredible stories that quickly engage the reader. Neal Childs shares deep wisdom that comes from a vast wealth of hands-on ministry in some of the most exciting and challenging places in the world. Neal, Danette, and their amazing family are favorites at our church where they inspire all to believe that we can partner with a miracle working God to change the world.

Dr. Bill Shuler
Capital Life Church, Senior Pastor

Generational thinking. Discipleship. Spiritual fatherhood. Future proofing the ministry. These are not ideas or theological concepts understood by many within modern day evangelicalism. However, not only has Neal Childs experienced it, he understands it and he lives it - and fortunately for the rest of us he has written a book about it "Beyond One".

Messiah gave us the great commission to make disciples. This was not the great suggestion or an optional extra to the Christian experience, but the paradigm needed that would transform the individual and change the world. Neal's book not only will lead you on a personal journey of discovering this paradigm but will introduce you to the wonderful world doing bible things in bible ways.

Dr. Scott Stewart
Agape Church, Senior Pastor

I have been privileged to watch Neal and Danette live out this life message. It is a message the Church needs to embrace. Like me, you will be inspired to think and live with generational purpose.

Steve Miner
Cornerstone Christian, Lead Pastor

As a seasoned missionary, Rev. Neal Childs has penned what he believes and practices. **BEYOND ONE** is original, a word from the heart of the Father God to us His children to make His glorious name known to the oncoming generation. The baton must be passed on and on till Jesus comes.

Psalm 22:31 – *His righteous acts will be told to those yet unborn. They will hear about everything he has done. (NLT)*

Rev. Koyejo Amori
Vie Abondante, Missionary to Niger

If I wanted to give someone a neat and biblically based book on generational thinking it would be this. Pastor Neal Childs, missionary and missionary son has done an admirable job in simplifying the complex process of generational thinking. Without looking for stories in distant countries, we must be very clear that God has a thought for the generation that will come after us. The question we have to ask ourselves is, "What can we do now so that we can influence the coming generation?"

Rev. Moctar Soumana
Vie Abondante – Eagle's Chapel, Pastor

BEYOND ONE is an awakening to our present generation - a knowledge impartation to those who are ignorant of the next-generation mind set. Every leader should read this book because it will help you to be conscious of next generation. The messages of this book are not theory but born out of many years of practical experience with undeniable results of which I am an eyewitness.

Rev. Nelson Nwene
International Christian Fellowship, Pastor

BEYOND ONE is a fantastic book, an absolute must read! Neal Childs, the author, challenges the reader to move from a place of selfish and introspective living to a place of thinking and operating generationally. Throughout the book you will be blessed and confronted with truths that could radically change your daily activities and worldview. Numerous power-packed statements like, *"The very meaning of the word 'succeed' indicates the necessity of continuation"* made me want to put the book down immediately and begin investing more time, energy, and resources into my biological and spiritual sons and daughters. By the time you have finished the book you will have found yourself engaged in a new way of doing life and thinking in terms of generations and legacy!

Jason Holland
Joshua Nations, President

BEYOND ONE struck such a strong chord in my heart that has been resonating for years – the importance of building ministry with a generational mindset. We have all heard and may have even experienced the failure of ministry leaders who didn't finish strong and pass on to the next generation the work God had called them to steward. What does it profit someone to have initial perceived success, yet fail by not preparing the next generation to continue the work beyond what they could accomplish? Like it's been said, "may our ceiling of success be the floor the next generation builds upon."

This practical journey lived out in the pages of **BEYOND ONE** isn't theory! It's been tried through the fiery trials of the highs and lows of ministry in a very difficult context – Niger, Africa. The lessons in this book have come out of a life rooted and grounded in a deep relationship with Christ and lived out in the family. Although many of the stories are from a missions context, the principles Neal imparts will traverse into any context you have been called.

Miles L. Phelps
City for the Nations, Executive Director

Dedicated to the works of the Kingdom, even in remote areas of the country, Rev. Neal Childs, an American missionary, has often renounced the comfort of the capital to live, with his family, in local regions, where he shared the gospel in a fluent Hausa. From the south of Nigeria to the far ends of Niger, Rev. Neal Childs, during his entire life, showed faithfulness and consistency in preaching the Good News. Recalling his unique experience, I am reminded of the verse from the Holy Bible: "Then I heard the voice of the Lord saying, "*Whom shall I send? And who will go for us?*" And I said, "*Here am I. Send me!*" (Isaiah 6:8-9).

Beyond One: a generational approach to life and ministry summarizes the difficult and complex situations he encountered and takes us to another dimension to understand the leadership secrets, the determination, and the revelations to walk us through the Great Commission. I recommend this book to all servants who desire to understand the living realities of having a ready heart for the Mission.

Bishop Kimso Boureima
Bethel World Outreach Ministries International, Niger

Dr. Kat and Mr. David,

May your children go
higher!

June 2020

Neal

BEYOND ONE

*a generational approach to
leadership & ministry*

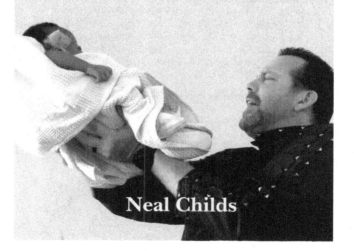

Neal Childs

Beyond One
A Generational Approach to Life and Ministry

Copyright © 2020 by Neal Childs

Printed in the United States of America

First Printing, 2020

ISBN 979-8-6495364-8-6

Cover Design: Danette Childs

www.runintl.org

Scripture quotations marked *NIV* are:
Scripture taken from the HOLY BIBLE, NEW INTERNATIONAL VERSION®. Copyright © 1973, 1978, 1984 Biblica. Used by permission of Zondervan. All rights reserved. The "NIV" and "New International Version" trademarks are registered in the United States Patent and Trademark Office by Biblica. Use of either trademark requires the permission of Biblica.

Scripture quotations marked *NKJV* are:
Scripture taken from the New King James Version®. Copyright © 1982 by Thomas Nelson, Inc. Used by permission. All rights reserved.

Scripture quotations marked *TPT* are:
Scripture quotations marked TPT are from The Passion Translation®. Copyright © 2017, 2018 by Passion & Fire Ministries, Inc. Used by permission. All rights reserved. ThePassionTranslation.com.

Scripture quotations marked *KJV* are:
Scripture taken from the King James Version.

All scriptures with **emphasis added** is by author.

Dedication

Dedicated to the generations of my family:

My Great-Grandpa Carter who made me my first slingshot, using the tongue of one of his shoes for the leather pouch.

My Grandpa Childs who I refer to in the book and who instilled in me a passion for travel when he gave me my first foreign coin collection.

My Grandma Childs from whom I think I inherited a love for games.

My Grandpa Sasser who often took me to the park to feed the ducks. He would even go down the circle slide with me.

My Grandma Louise who inspired the feisty side in me. It has served me well in tough situations.

My Dad and Mom who are legendary in West Africa and whom I share more details in the chapters.

My son, Trae, who is a leader and a great father to his four children.

My daughter, Tanika, who sets the standard when it comes to determination.

My son, Tobi, who people always want to be around.

And last but not least, my grandchildren: Judah, Charlie, Desmond, Levi, and Oliver.

Acknowledgments

My wife, Danette, is amazing. Her encouragement and support have inspired me to get the message of generational thinking into a book. Without her suggestions, edits, and help, it would not have been completed.

I want to also acknowledge our partners that make it possible for us to be serving in Niger. Because of our partners, new converts have been discipled, churches have been planted, and pastors have been trained. They have demonstrated the generational commitment that the Great Commission demands.

I am grateful for the RUN International Board of Directors that have offered their guidance and encouragement.

I am also grateful for the pastors and leaders of Vie Abondante that I have had the privilege of serving with for the past 22 years. They are strong, full of faith, and committed to the Great Commission.

Lastly, I appreciate my brother-in-law, Scott Lout. He has given of his time and talents to help me edit this book despite a swamped schedule. Thanks, Bro!

Contents

Forward

We live in such a schedule-driven world, that life always seems focused on the immediate tasks at hand. "Staying relevant" is a battle fought by age groups at the cost of their own significance & value. What we impart beyond our brief moments here, whether to our natural or spiritual sons and daughters, is embedded in the true cause. In the continuity of greater generational thinking comes the greater grace, an enlarging of a tent that requires humility and the absence of pride. Disconnect in the generations because of fear & insecurity can no longer be called fathering.

This epidemic is in ministry because our culture is sadly filled with poor relationships with absent fathers, the vacuum filling with dishonor and competition. These were not the days of Jesus' discipleship. But beautifully modeled in Neal's life and family is his ability to walk with his own father in ministry while training his sons and daughter after him, including the founders in the whole family and ministry process.

Their whole presence in the desert looks more like Abraham than anyone I know! These are authentic spiritual leaders who have taught my daughter in school, who have stayed in my home (Neal and John contending *fiercely at the Chess board for hours), me spending hot days in their home... I assure you Neal Childs is qualified to tell his compelling stories and to challenge yours.*

Cathie Dorsch
Commission Fields, Founder
Author, Motivational Speaker
*Host and Producer of **"Kids Like You"** television show*

Introduction

We have all heard Jesus' last words before ascending to heaven in front of the disciples, "Go into all the world and preach the Gospel to all creation." This is known as the **Great Commission**. It's *"Great"* because it is given by the highest authority and is of the highest priority. It is a *"mission"* because it is a sending forth to fulfill the task given by the Lord Jesus. And by Jesus statements, it is a *"Commission"* because He has assured us that He is working together with us as we go forth into all the world.

It is the Great Commission that has compelled generations of missionaries to go forth and lay down their lives for the sake of reaching all people with the Good News of Jesus. It is the Great Commission that has compelled the Church to give and make the sacrifices necessary to cross borders, cultures, and languages with the Gospel. It is the Great Commission that compels us today to do whatever it takes to get the Good News of Jesus to all the peoples of the earth. The failure to fulfill this command results in many more people dying and going to hell. That is the harsh truth of the Great Commission.

During my time serving in Africa as a missionary among unreached people, I have come to the realization that the Great Commission requires both a *missional* approach and a *generational* approach. We often emphasize the importance of *going*. To be missional is about going - to be sending or to be sent. This is the heart of the Great Commission. But we must also, in addition to being missional, be generational.

Generational thinking is at the heart of Jesus teachings and is necessary for us in our responsibility of carrying out the Great Commission. My purpose in writing this book is to highlight the necessity of generational thinking and show it imperative to fulfilling the Great Commission.

Generation - all *of the people born and living at about the same time, regarded collectively.*[1]

There is much discussion of what a generation means in terms of years. Since a generation is the period *during which children are born and grow up, become adults, and begin to have their own children*, it is commonly understood to be about 30 years.[2]

4

From a Biblical perspective, there are several timeframes that can be supported. From God's words to Abraham in Genesis 15 concerning the 400 years that his descendants would be "strangers in a country not their own" to a study of the generations of Abraham's descendants in Egypt, there are three numbers of years that are typically accepted as a Biblical generation: 100, 40, and 70.[3]

From a technological perspective, the generations seem to be closing in on each other. You can hardly walk out of an electronics store with the latest and greatest device and have it last more than a month before it is on the verge of being obsolete. The next version has already been designed, tested and is waiting to be released.

The principles I am highlighting in this book are not dependent on a particular length of time for a generation. Rather, it is the collective group of people born and living at the same time that is most relevant when considering a generational approach to life and ministry.

Recorded in the scriptures are numerous passages dedicated to the recording of lineages. While we may often jump ahead as we wade through what seems to be endless genealogies, we must recognize that there is a significance to including these in God's Holy Word. Not only do they preserve the historical timeline of the human race, they show our God to be mindful of the generations. Our God is a God of generations. *"How great are His signs, And how mighty His wonders! His kingdom is an everlasting kingdom, And His dominion is from generation to generation"* (Dan. 4:3).

Chapter One

Always Another

Judges 2:10 – *"All that generation also were gathered to their fathers; and **there arose another generation after them** who did not know the Lord, nor yet the works which He had done for Israel."* KJV

There will always be another generation. God's word has assured us of this in Genesis 8:22 when it tells us that "while the earth remains, seedtime and harvest, cold and heat, summer and winter, day and night will never cease." The seasons will continue, reproduction will continue, and the generations will continue. Generational thinking begins with an understanding that there will always be another generation.

We cannot be so short-sighted that we only live for today. We must learn to think beyond the day-to-day and consider the seasons. And we must learn to think beyond the seasons and consider the generations. We cannot think inside the bubble of a single generation and expect that we will obtain a witness for the Gospel in every nation. As long as the earth remains, there will always be another generation. And with every generation people are born needing to hear the message that we have been commissioned to give. We must begin to think generationally if we are going to obey the command of preaching the Gospel to all creation.

I remember vividly, as a child, walking through a cemetery and noticing the various types of headstones and reading the different inscriptions. They represented those who had already lived. Their times had now passed. As a young person, I found it difficult to understand the passing of time or how to accurately gauge time. It seemed that my parents, my teachers, or really, any of the adults in my life, were so very old. A generation seemed like forever. I felt as if I had all the time in the world. Without an awareness of a ticking clock on the length of our lives, it is easy to only see the here and now.

We can get so focused on the day to day that we easily forget that there is a world that has existed for many generations before us. And even more significantly, there are generations that will continue after us. Modern times have brought a speed of life that seems to have lessened our awareness that we are only a chapter in a story that extends to many generations.

My wife, Danette, and I learned quickly on the mission field that another generation is right around the corner. We had only been serving in The Republic of Niger for a few months when we started a children's ministry with a purpose of reaching out to the broader community, in the border town of Maradi, just north of Nigeria. Cima, a fourteen-year-old girl, prayed with us to receive Jesus on one of her first visits to the children's service. It was not long after this that Cima asked to be water baptized. It was clearly a significant and wonderful time of spiritual awakening in this young girl's life.

A few months later we were asked by a young man in one of the village churches to help him with the dowry so that he could marry Cima. Of course, we thought this was absurd as she was hardly 15 years old. Being relatively new to the culture at that time, we were just starting to become aware of how prevalent the disturbing practice of child marriages were in Niger. As of 2017, 28% of the girls are married before the age of 15.[1] As opposed as we were to child marriage, when we realized the situation, we were convinced to give toward the dowry. Her family was ready to give her to a much older Muslim suitor who was ready to pay the dowry immediately. So Cima, at 15, was married.

We were honored to be a significant part of Cima's wedding when she married Ishaya, a Christian brother who was preparing to be trained as a pastor. A year later we dedicated their first baby in the church. It was Cima's daughter coming into the children's service that was most impacting to me.

From Cima getting saved in our children's ministry, water baptized, married, dedicating her baby, to having her little girl in the children's service, we had seen an entire generational cycle in a few short years. Today she and her husband, with their six children, pastor a new church plant among an unreached people group in Niger. There will always be another generation.

What we do today does impact tomorrow. We may not be able to change history, but the future is in our hands. We may not eat the fruit of the trees we plant, but our children and our children's children will. Psalm 127:4 tells us that our children are "like arrows in the hands of a warrior." We must release and launch the next generation. Like arrows that are sent forth, our children will go forward and reach beyond our days.

Our God is a God of generations. He is called the God of Abraham, Isaac, and Jacob. His plans span generations. His words to Abraham speak of many generations when He says to Abraham, "in you shall all the nations of the earth be blessed." God tells Abraham in Genesis 17 that He made Abraham the father of many nations -- that He was establishing His covenant between Himself, Abraham, and Abraham's descendants throughout their generations for an everlasting covenant. Jesus, the express image of God, is the same yesterday, today, and forever. Our God is a God of generations and we too must think in terms of generations. It is not about the moment - it is about eternity. God has a plan that goes beyond. It is a plan of everlasting life.

After Moses, there was Joshua. After David, there was Solomon. After Elijah, there was Elisha. When we think it couldn't get any better, God raises up another to remind us that His story – one built on generational thinking - is not over. Who could ever follow in the footsteps of Moses? He spoke to God face to face as a man speaks to his friend. His face shone so bright with the glory of God that he had to wear a veil to interact with the people. But sure enough, God raised up another that could do what Moses could not. It was Joshua that God had prepared to lead the children of Israel into the Promised Land.

David, the brave young man who famously defeated the giant Goliath, went on to be known by many as Israel's greatest king. He was a man after God's own heart. And still another came after David who became known as the wisest man in all the earth, King Solomon. The wisest and wealthiest of kings, Solomon's exploits are unparalleled.

Elijah has been referred to as the most beloved prophet in the Bible. He was known as a miracle worker, an inspirational leader of his time, possessing authority to hold back the clouds of rain, and finally, to be carried away by God in a whirlwind. Again, God raised up a successor to Elijah who would receive a double portion of the anointing that was on him. Elisha has twice the number of miracles recorded in scripture than Elijah.

There will always be another generation. And with God, it keeps getting better. In Isaiah 43:18, it says, "remember not the former things, nor consider the things of old. Behold I am doing a new thing." When we look at this passage in its context, God is telling the people of Israel that the best is yet to come. He is essentially telling them to stop looking back to the great days of Moses and Joshua, and to know that the best days are ahead. Even greater works lay in the generations still to come. There will always be another generation.

Chapter Two

Tell Your Story

Judges 2:10 – *"All that generation also were gathered to their fathers; and there arose another generation after them* **who did not know the Lord, nor yet the works which He had done for Israel.***" KJV*

It is an amazing tragedy that the generation immediately following Joshua's death did not know the Lord. They didn't know the stories or the awesome miracles that God had done for Israel just a few years earlier.

One of my greatest joys has been to tell my children about my childhood. To share with them the incredible adventures that I had growing up in Nigeria has always been at the top of my 'parenthood' list. Living in a remote village with no running water or electricity and learning to adapt in a different culture, provided interesting stories for my children. Telling them of my first-hand experience of an apostolic move of God through my childhood pastor, Archbishop Benson Idahosa, was not only my story to tell, but my responsibility to pass on. It was a responsibility and a privilege to share these stories with my children that I might steer them in a direction that I had been assured of through my own experiences.

I fondly remember taking them to Benin City where my parents served as missionaries. I told my children about the miracle healing crusades that I had witnessed as a young boy. To have experienced such awesome and supernatural moments in my life and not have shared them with my children, would have kept them from truly knowing *me*. More importantly, they would have missed out on understanding the testimonies of God's favor in my life – a critical foundation of which they might build upon.

The unintentional neglect of thinking generationally has a hefty price tag. There are devastating consequences for disregarding the importance of a generational mentality. Israel failed to ensure that the wonderful stories of the greatest rescue from slavery ever recorded in history were passed on to the next generation. It is hard to imagine that the miraculous events God orchestrated for Israel through the hands of Moses and Joshua were unknown to the very next generation. What a tragedy that, after God had unleashed His power through ten plagues, split the Red Sea, miraculously fed Israel with bread from heaven, stopped the flow of the Jordan River, brought the Israelites into a land *flowing with milk and honey,* that the next generation would not know the Lord nor the awesome works that He had done for them. That is a catastrophe from which we must learn. We must be next generation minded and ensure that the testimonies of God's favor on us are passed on to those coming after us.

Israel continued to suffer the fate of generational disconnect. They failed again and again to effectively pass on the ways of the Lord to the next generation. Throughout the Old Testament we see Israel in a cycle of sin, bondage, deliverance, and freedom. Unfortunately, after each time Israel finds themselves delivered through God's intervention, they fail to pass on to the next generation the critical advice and direction to keep them from repeating their mistakes.

God had even warned Israel of the importance of passing on to the next generation the testimonies of what God had done. He instructed the Israelites in Joshua chapter 4 to have a man from each of the twelve tribes take a stone from the Jordan River – the same river He had miraculously stopped on their behalf as they crossed into the Promised Land. God said they were to use these stones to build a memorial, so that in the times to come, when the children would ask 'what does this mean?,' Israel would tell them the stories of God's mighty works in leading them into their Promised Land.

This is an example of building a building without telling the story. In other words, a church building without a shepherd teaching God's Word will not produce fruit that remains. The building alone does not guarantee a future. Our legacy must be more than a building. We must tell the stories of God's favor to our children.

Psalm 78:4 *"We've heard the true stories from our fathers about our rich heritage. We will continue to tell our children and not hide from the rising generation the great marvels of our God – His miracles and power that have brought us all this far."* *TPT*

We cannot assume that they will understand by what they see with their eyes. They must also hear from our mouths if we are going to successfully pass on our heritage of faith to the next generation.

In 2 Chronicles chapter 34, we see eight-year-old Josiah installed as one of the youngest kings to sit on the throne of Israel. His young age was not an obstacle for him to do what was right in the eyes of the Lord. Even in his youth, Josiah gave instruction to collect money from the treasury and renovate the house of God. It was in those renovations of the temple that the Book of the Law was found. Apparently, it had been lost. Imagine that the Book of the Law, God's Word, given to God's chosen people for their blessing and prosperity, was simply misplaced in the temple. It was only to be found because of the "off chance" that some renovations were being carried out.

The people had since forgotten the words of the Lord. The story tells us that the book was found and brought to King Josiah. And when he heard the words of the book being read aloud to him, he tore his robes and said, "Great is the Lord's anger that is poured out on us because those who have gone before us have not kept the word of the Lord" (2 Chr. 34:21). King Josiah led them to celebrate the Passover in a way that "had not been observed like this in Israel since the days of the prophet Samuel" (2 Chr. 35:18). Sometimes we need to renovate the house of God. Sometimes we need to renovate our own house. We need to make sure that we are not allowing our heritage of faith to be forgotten nor our legacy lost.

America's 40th President, Ronald Reagan, was well loved and known for his contribution to the winning of the Cold War resulting in the demise of Soviet communism. Reagan made a statement during his presidency that underscores the significant consequences associated with not having generational thinking. He said, *"Freedom is never more than a generation away from extinction. We didn't pass it to our children in the bloodstream. It must be fought for, protected, and handed on for them to do the same."*[1]

The heritage of our faith is no less vulnerable. It is not automatically passed on through DNA, it must be taught. The stories must be told. The truths must be protected. And yes, it may even be a fight. But it is a fight worth fighting. May it never be said whether in our families, our homes, or in our churches, that the next generation did not know the Lord nor the mighty works that He had done.

Chapter Three

Think Beyond One

Proverbs 13:22 – *"A good man leaves an inheritance to his children's children, but the wealth of the sinner is stored up for the righteous."* *NKJV*

A good man leaves an inheritance to his children's children. Thinking beyond a single generation is not only heralded as good, but it is expressed in contrast to sin. The wisdom of this proverb teaches the importance of generational thinking. Generational thinking goes beyond one generation. Thinking beyond one generation not only requires a generous measure of preparation, it requires an intentional pursuit.

My grandfather was a good man. When he died in 1991, he left an inheritance to his children. The inheritance included land, a vehicle, a couple of houses, and money. He also left each of his grandchildren $5,000. So all those years ago, I received an inheritance of $5,000. As I said, my grandfather was a good man. The Bible says so.

An inheritance can be money, land, houses, cars, or anything of value that is passed on to those you are leaving behind. While it is awesome to receive an inheritance of money or various properties, the greatest inheritance that you can ever leave to your children, and your children's children, is the knowledge of Jesus Christ as Lord and Savior. The heritage of your faith should be understood as the highest valued possession that you could ever pass on to those you leave behind.

In these modern times there seems to be less of an awareness of preparing for future generations. With life moving so fast with cell phones, internet, and speedy and convenient transportation options, people are forced to stay focused on the immediate tasks at hand. The pressure to stay relevant to the moment in our fast-moving society and quickly changing world seems to have blurred the significance of generational thinking.

Like most missionaries we try to stay up to date on the latest ministry strategies by reading books and articles pertaining to world missions. From time to time we may even have opportunities to attend missions conferences where experts in our field share their knowledge, inspiring us to fulfill our calling as those that have been sent. 'One-liner' quotes that capture a truth are a common technique for inspiring action needed for the task of world missions. Over the years, I have come across several that have touched me deeply. Some of my favorites are:

"Why should anyone hear the Gospel twice before everyone has heard it once?"[1]

- Oswald Smith

"We talk of the Second Coming; half the world has never heard of the first."[2]

- Oswald Smith

"To know the will of God, we need an open Bible and an open map."[3]

- William Carey

"The mark of a great church is not its seating capacity, but its sending capacity."[4]

- Mike Stachura

"Christ alone can save the world, but Christ cannot save the world alone."[5]

- David Livingstone

The vast majority of missions one-liners are powerful quotes that inspire us, mobilize us to action and keep our focus on the missional expectation of the Great Commission. However, one quote I heard did not sit right with me.

"This generation can only reach this generation!"[6]

- David Livingstone

When I heard that statement, I understood its purpose. It was clearly a motivational sound bite to galvanize its hearers to action. And while I completely agree with the sentiment that there is a great work that has been left undone and requires those who are here now to take immediate action, I disagree with its subtle narrow scope with which to approach the mission. The statement lacks revelation of generational thinking. It voids the contributions of countless laborers who continue to reach people long past their days on earth. It takes for granted the stage which this generation has been given.

We must understand that today does impact tomorrow. And while we cannot change history, we can certainly change the future. What we do today will have consequences that far outlast our brief moments on earth. And we must know that what we do today is on the shoulders of those who have gone before us. We must think generationally. We must reject the tendency toward a single-generation mindset.

My first visit to Paris, France, made me realize how young the United States is as a nation. It gave me a better perspective of time. I was amazed when we toured the Notre Dame Cathedral and learned that it took almost 200 years to build just the first phase. Its construction spanned lifetimes, generations, and even centuries. Imagine the architects, masons, and craftsmen starting the job and never seeing its completion. Many great works of human ingenuity have required generational commitment.

It is easy today to take for granted that we can hold meetings at night because we have lights. Thomas Edison is not from this generation. We enjoy speaking to large crowds with powerful sound systems. These are not tools that came from this generation. Airplanes, automobiles, computers, the internet and many books and study materials have been laid up for us from previous generations. We must realize that what we do today is on the shoulders of those who have gone before us. Our successes are, in fact, their successes.

If there is anything to be recognized as a vital component for our success in the work of the Great Commission, it is the Holy Bible. And the Bible, which we carry in our hands, have loaded on our phones, and is in almost every language on the earth, is not a product of this generation. Men of past years, like John Wycliffe and William Tyndale, gave up their lives, being persecuted and killed in order for us to have Bibles in our languages today.[7]

It was in a meeting, shortly before moving to Niger as missionaries, that a prophetic word was spoken over us. We had spent the previous ten months traveling to churches and raising our financial support. We had met many new friends who had embraced our vision and were ready to "launch" us off to reach the unreached. The prophetic word was given from John chapter 4.

John 4:37-38 *"Thus the saying 'One sows and another reaps' is true. I sent you to reap what you have not worked for. Others have done the work, and you have reaped the benefits of their labor." NIV*

In the 22 years since that encouraging word was spoken over us, we have certainly seen it come to pass. And just as it was spoken, we reaped where we had not even sown. One sows and another reaps. It is encouraging and it is humbling. We must know that our victories are often realized because of those who have worked hard before us. While we reap what we sow, we also reap what others have prepared in advance for us.

We cannot afford to think, plan, and execute in a vacuum of a single-generation mindset. We must begin to think beyond the limitation of our lifespan. We must begin to ensure that our work is going to live long past our years spent on this planet. We need a generational commitment in how we plan, prepare, and develop missions strategies.

Chapter Four

Next Generation Mentality

Genesis 18:17-19 – *"And the Lord said, "Shall I hide from Abraham that thing which I do; Seeing that Abraham shall surely become a great and mighty nation, and all the nations of the earth shall be blessed in him? For I know him,* **that he will command his children and his household after him, and they shall keep the way of the Lord, to do justice and judgment;** *that the Lord may bring upon Abraham that which He hath spoken of him."* KJV

The Lord knew that He could trust Abraham with His plans because Abraham was next generation minded. Abraham understood the importance of generational thinking. Abraham understood that it was not just about what he would do in his lifetime, but what his children would do. The Lord indicates in these verses that it was this kind of multi-generational mentality that gave Him the confidence to trust Abraham. Just as God entrusted to Abraham His covenant plans for man's redemption, God searches for men and women today who are next generation minded with whom He may entrust to carry out His plans.

Abraham was next generation minded. From the moment he is mentioned in the Bible, he is associated with generations. When the Lord first speaks to him in Genesis, God tells Abraham that in him "all the families of the earth shall be blessed" (Gen.12:3). His name, which God had actually changed from Abram to Abraham, literally means "father of many nations," underscoring his generational mentality.

During one of the early conversations that Abraham had with the Lord, he asked God about his next generation and who might inherit his estate. It is at that time God told Abraham to count the stars, indicating to Abraham how numerous his offspring would be. God's plans extend beyond one generation. Abraham's focus and concern for a successor should serve as an example for us today.

We need this next generation mindset if we are going to be connected to what God began to do yesterday, is doing today, and will forever continue to do, until His plans are fulfilled. God is a God of generations. And His plans are achieved in a generational progression. For "He who began a good work in you will carry it on to completion until the day of Christ Jesus" (Phil 1:6).

God blessed Abraham. God made his name great. God blessed those who blessed Abraham and cursed those who cursed Abraham. God made a covenant with Abraham as a confirmation of a promised land that would be given to him and his descendants. God's blessings over Abraham were directly correlated to Abraham's devotion to the continuation of their special covenant through future generations. There was a generational responsibility for Abraham to teach, train, and instill the covenant truths to his children.

The significance of imparting the way of the Lord to our children must be our priority. The importance of teaching our children is seen throughout scripture. In Deuteronomy chapter 6, God instructs Israel with what Jesus later tells us in Matthew chapter 22 to be the greatest commandment:

"Love the Lord your God with all your heart and with all your soul and with all your strength." ***Deut. 6:5 NIV***

And then, after God has commanded the people of Israel to keep these words in their heart, He says:

"Impress them on your children. Talk about them when you sit at home and when you walk along the road, when you lie down and when you get up." ***Deut. 6:7 NIV***

We see that the greatest commandment to love God is immediately followed by the command to make sure our children know it and live it. Passing our heritage of faith on to our children is God's plan. He expects the raising of our children in the knowledge and fear of the Lord to be our priority. Generational thinking is not just an optional approach to life, but a mandate given by God to carry out His plan to reach all nations.

In the New Testament, we see that the raising of our children is so important that the criteria for church leadership is based on "having his children in submission with all reverence" (I Tim 3:4). It is not about a leader's gifts, abilities, and accomplishments as much as it is about his testimony regarding his children that qualifies him to be in church leadership.

Leadership requires generational thinking. A common leadership principle says, **"Success without a successor is failure."**[1] The sentiment here is that no matter how great an impact you may make while you are in a position, if it does not continue after you, it is a failure.

True success has a lasting impact. True success extends beyond a single generation. The very meaning of the word "succeed" indicates the necessity of continuation.

"Succeed" means **"to have success"** like in the sentence,

"If I work hard, I will succeed."

But it also means **"to come after"** like in the sentence,

"Joshua was to succeed Moses when He died."

Our success is not just based on the impact we make while we are in a position, but on how our impact continues after we are out of that position. Success is seen in the perpetuation of our purpose and in the transition to another. Our influence goes beyond our time.

Success may mean different things to different people. By definition, success is based on achievement, or in other words, achieving certain goals. The world's system often assumes that we all have the same goals: money, fame, power, and influence. But when we live by a different set of values, our understanding of success is also different. As Christians, success should be much more than a pursuit of money, fame, power, and influence. Success should be based on fulfilling God's purpose. Success should be measured by what God has created us for and called us to do. Living out God's unique plan and calling upon our lives as individuals is the only achievement worthy to be used for identifying success.

God is a God of generations. His plan goes beyond a single generation. Your success as a Christian requires generational thinking. It is about living out His plan for your life and passing that same example on to those following after you. Like Abraham, we must be next generation minded. Abraham could be trusted by God to raise his children to carry out God's plan. Our success to fulfilling God's plan for our individual lives is tied to being next generation minded. It requires generational commitment. Generational thinking and commitment must be intentional. We can choose our legacy.

Chapter Five

Empower to Higher Levels

John 14:12 – *"Most assuredly, I say to you, he who believes in Me, the works that I do he will do also; and **greater works than these he will do**, because I go to My Father." NKJV*

These words of Jesus to His disciples are extraordinary. Imagine Jesus, Son of God, who went about healing all manner of sickness, stunning the religious leaders with His wisdom and authoritative teaching, performing life changing miracles, and raising the dead, now tells his students that they will do the same. And not just the same, even greater!

While it is difficult to fully grasp the meaning and weight of this statement, it speaks clearly to the generational approach that Jesus used in His ministry. Only Jesus could do what Jesus did. He is the spotless lamb of God who takes away the sins of the world. No one else would ever be qualified or able to do what Jesus did. As indispensable as Jesus was for the work of redemption that he came to do, His key strategy was in raising up others. The majority of Jesus' time was spent in ministry to His disciples. From day one, He was about raising up those who would continue the work after His time was done, investing in those who would carry on His work into the next generation.

Jesus' example was not only to raise up the next generation, but to empower the next generation to live at a higher level and to be ready for even greater works. The next generation should never be limited by those responsible for raising them up.

I remember when I was growing up in Nigeria and I was getting close to the height of my father. I began to tell people, "I am going to be taller than my father." One day a Nigerian man overheard me saying this and proceeded to tell me,

"In Africa, a son is never taller than his father."

Now I understood his meaning and the point that he was making. We know that there is a healthy sense of honor and respect given to the elders in African cultures. And while I agree with the importance of honoring our fathers, I also know that as a father today, and even as a grandfather, I want my children to be taller than me. Or should I say, to go higher than me.

We should all desire for our children to go higher, for our children to have more, for our children to do more, and for our children to go further. Only a small man tries to hold his children down. Only an insecure leader holds down those whom he should empower and release to higher levels of influence. Yes, the sons must honor the fathers, but the fathers must empower the sons. May our *Elishas* have the double portion anointing!

When my oldest son was in college at Oral Roberts University, I came to the realization that he had surpassed me in almost everything. I too had been a student at ORU, and by my sophomore year I was put in a leadership position of RA (Resident Advisor) in the dormitory. It was not common for a second-year student to be named as RA. It was an honor for me to be given this responsibility.

One month, I was identified as 'RA of the Month.' This title was rewarded with a framed certificate and the honor of sharing a fancy meal with the Dean of Men. Well, my son, Trae, also chose to go to university at ORU. He also was identified into a leadership role of RA for his sophomore year. However, he did not receive the award for being 'RA of the Month.' Instead, he was awarded a plaque as 'RA of the Year!'

It was around that time, Trae and a friend had been invited by a church to train their mission team. The church flew them across the country, put them in a hotel, fed them some incredible seafood meals, and at the end of the weekend when they were taken to the airport to return, the church presented each of the young men an envelope. Trae told me that he waited until he was on the plane to open the envelope. Inside was a check for $1500. When I was a student, I was never invited to go train a church mission team. I was never given an envelope. And I certainly was never given a check for $1500!

Trae was married at 20 years old and had four kids by the time he was 28 years old. I didn't get married until the age of 23 and I have 3 kids. As of today, I have traveled to 39 countries. Trae has been to 44. I promise you, this is not a competition. But the truth is that Trae seems to have surpassed me in everything. Does that make me feel embarrassed or ashamed? Of course not! He is my son. His success is my success! As I share these accomplishments of Trae, I am proud. I am proud in the sense of being honored. I want people to know that my son has gone higher, done more, and gone further. Fathers should always take joy in seeing their children grow and excel.

Leaders who do not or cannot take joy in the success of their people should not be in leadership. Leaders should be intentional in seeing their people excel. They should desire that the people under their influence and care be raised up to a level of influence even above their own. Leaders should not strive to make followers. Leadership is not about demanding submissive followers to do only what they are told. Leadership is about raising up and empowering others to lead. Leaders produce leaders. The foundational revelation of generational thinking should inspire us to see that our children's successes are our successes.

Matthew 10:24 *"The **student is not above the teacher**, nor a servant above his master. It is enough for students to be like their teachers, and servants like their masters. If the head of the house has been called Beelzebul, how much more the members of his household!" NIV*

It was at a pastors' conference in Uganda where I had shared this message, that I was asked how my teaching on our "children going higher" correlated to Jesus' statement that "a disciple is not above his teacher." When we understand that our children's successes are our successes, we will never be less. As your child goes higher, and does works that are greater, you are, as the parent, just as much honored.

It is time for leaders to stop being intimidated by the next generation. Too often, leaders hold down those they should be lifting up. Insecurity deceives many leaders into thinking that by keeping others down they keep themselves up. Politics seems to work this way, but true leadership empowers. If leaders would think generationally, they would actually increase their influence, not decrease it. A leader is never less by reproducing himself.

Jesus reproduced Himself in His disciples. He was not afraid to lift up His disciples. He was not afraid to empower His disciples. He even gave them credit for greater works than his. Jesus spoke this prophesy over His disciples before they were demonstrating an admirable example of faith. Our children will not always do the right thing, but that should never stop us from working with them, encouraging them, and empowering them.

In Mark chapter 16, just one verse before committing to them the massive responsibility of the Great Commission, Jesus rebuked His disciples. A full-on rebuke for unbelief and hardness of heart immediately before committing to them the greatest leadership roles seen in the church's history. Fathers in the faith must stop hiding behind the excuses that their sons and daughters are not ready for leadership.

Chapter Six

Never Abandon

2 Kings 20:1-3 *"In those days Hezekiah was sick and near death. And Isaiah the prophet, the son of Amoz, went to him and said to him, 'Thus says the Lord: 'Set your house in order, for you shall die, and not live.' Then he turned his face toward the wall, and prayed to the Lord, saying, 'Remember now, O Lord, I pray, how I have walked before you in truth and with a loyal heart, and done what is good in Your sight.' And Hezekiah wept bitterly." NKJV*

Hezekiah was sick. The passage tells us that he was on his death bed when he receives a word from the Lord. This word from the Lord is direct and clear, leaving no room for misunderstanding, saying that he needs to get his affairs in order because he is going to die. Despite the fact that this word is from almighty God, creator of heaven and earth, Hezekiah cries out to God pleading for his fate to be changed. The passage details to us how passionately he pleads his case reminding the Lord of his good testimony, even to the extent of weeping bitterly.

In the following verses we see that the Lord has heard Hezekiah's prayers, has seen his tears, and adds to his life fifteen years. This is an amazing story showing the power of prayer. I have heard messages on 'prayer changing the heart of God' based on this story. The passage certainly gives us insight into how effective the prayers of God's people can be. Hezekiah had served the Lord as a righteous king and found favor from the Lord. Just as James 3:16 tells us that "the effective, fervent prayer of a righteous man avails much," Hezekiah's prayers had a major impact on his life. The older I get the more I appreciate and realize how significant it is to have fifteen years added to a man's life.

Moving forward in this same chapter, we see that the word of the Lord comes to Hezekiah a second time. This time the word of the Lord is not about his life but about those of his children – the next generation.

2 Kings 20:16-18 *"Then Isaiah said to Hezekiah, 'Hear the word of the Lord: Behold, the days are coming when all that is in your house, and what your fathers have accumulated until this day, shall be carried to Babylon; nothing shall be left, says the Lord. And they shall take away some of your sons who will descend from you, whom you will beget; and they shall be eunuchs in the palace of the king of Babylon.'" NKJV*

The word of the Lord spoke about what was coming to the next generation. Hezekiah was being made aware by the Lord of an attack that was to take place against his family and his descendants. All of the family inheritance passed down and accumulated from previous generations was going to be stolen and pillaged. Nothing of his heritage would be left. The attackers would even carry his sons away into slavery. Ultimately, Hezekiah's legacy would be forever cut off as his sons would be made eunuchs, never to reproduce again.

And how does Hezekiah respond?

2 Kings 20:19 *"So Hezekiah said to Isaiah, 'Good is the word of the Lord which thou hast spoken.' And he said, 'Is it not good, if peace and truth be in my days?'" KJV*

What? The message of annihilation of the next generation is something to be considered as good? Where is his fight? Where is the passionate crying out for his own children?

It is staggering to see the contrast of how Hezekiah responds to the word of the Lord that came regarding his life and personal situation to that of his descendants, the next generation. His attitude could be summed up as one of complete apathy. We must never allow this kind of thinking to infect our minds. No matter how great and righteous King Hezekiah had been for Israel, he blew it here. God was giving him a window into what was coming, and rather than fight for the next generation, he considered only his own life and had the audacity to say, "this is good."

When it was his life on the line, Hezekiah passionately cried out until he hurt, but when the word pertained to the next generation, he had no prayers to give. May we never be guilty of abandoning the next generation. What might have the plight of Israel been had Hezekiah chosen to cry out to God? Hezekiah lacked the generational mindset that would have surely pushed him to advocate for his children.

We must not allow selfishness to sabotage our children's destiny. When we lack generational thinking, we only see what is front of us. In fact, we only see ourselves. It is easy to succumb to a self-centered existence. Without a next generation mentality, a culture of selfishness subtly becomes our "normal."

Jesus' parable of the rich fool in Luke 12 also exposes the selfish mindset as being in direct opposition to generational thinking.

Luke 12:16-21 *"And he told them this parable: The ground of a certain rich man yielded an abundant harvest. He thought to himself, 'What shall I do? I have no place to store my crops.' Then he said, 'This is what*

I'll do. I will tear down my barns and build bigger ones,
and there I will store my surplus grain. And I'll say to
myself, You have plenty of grain laid up for many years.
Take life easy; eat, drink and be merry.' And God said to
him, 'You fool! This very night your life will be demanded
from you. Then who will get what you have prepared for
yourself?' This is how it will be with whoever stores up
things for themselves but is not rich toward God." NIV

Jesus called the rich man a fool because he only stored up for himself. He did not consider God. It says he was not rich toward God, but only stored up for himself. His actions and words also give away the fact that he had no plan for the next generation. There is no talk of his children, his community nor anyone other than himself.

The parable is told in such a way that it clearly shows the man to be self-absorbed and only concerned with his own well-being. In the few sentences used to tell the parable, the rich man refers to himself eight times:

- what shall I do
- I have no place
- to store my crops
- this is what I will do
- I will tear down and build bigger
- I will store
- my surplus grain
- I will say
- to myself

41

It is easy to identify the ego of the rich fool. However, we should stop and listen to ourselves from time to time. When we hear ourselves using first-person pronouns in most communication, we should really consider the content and focus of our message. Our words are a good indicator of what is in our hearts. Jesus tells us in Matthew 12:34 that "out of the abundance of the heart the mouth speaks."

A selfish mindset is not only in opposition to generational thinking, it is in direct opposition to the Agape love by which we find our identity as disciples of Jesus. "By this all men will know that you are my disciples, if you have love for one another" (John 13:35). And we know from I Corinthians 13:5 that Agape love "does not seek its own." As Jesus disciples, we "deny ourselves and take up our cross daily" (Luke 9:23). "We present ourselves unto God a living sacrifice which is our reasonable service" (Rom 12:1).

Selfishness is often the root cause that keeps us from seeing God's purpose fulfilled in our lives. We must make the sacrifices necessary to pass the baton of God's purpose to the next generation. Many have gone before us and paid the price so that today we can live in God's blessing of freedom, salvation, and revelation.

Hezekiah was so relieved that the calamity to befall his people would not touch him that he forgot about the power of his own prayer that had extended the days of his life on earth. He was so wrapped up in his own well-being that he did not cry out for the next generation. We must not abandon our children. We must never neglect to cry out for our children's salvation, protection, and blessing. No matter how bad the situation our children may be in, we can cry out to God. Prayer works. Prayer changes situations.

May our children go higher than we have gone. May our children live better than we have lived. May our children do more than we have done. May our children go further than we have gone. May our children have more than we have. We pray today for the next generation. We cry out for the purposes of God to be fulfilled in their lives. The calling of God on their lives will come to pass in Jesus name!

Chapter Seven

Fruit That Remains

John 15:16 – *"You did not choose Me, but I chose you and appointed you that you should go and bear fruit, and **that your fruit should remain,** that whatever you ask the Father in my name he may give you."* NKJV

Bearing fruit is a natural result of being alive. It is the natural result of being connected to the source. Bearing fruit is the passing forward of who we are. Bearing fruit is the manifestation of being generational. Jesus' words qualify this expectation to bear fruit with a very specific clarification. We are not to simply bear fruit, but to bear *'fruit that remains.'*

Fruit that remains is fruit that is reproducing. It is multi-generational. It is sustained. Some Bible translations use other words for "remain" so that it reads: "that your fruit will <u>abide</u>" or "that your fruit will <u>last</u>." The message being conveyed is that the fruits of our labor are not to be one generation deep, but should continue forward generationally, reproducing after its kind.

From the beginning God established the principle of reproducing 'after its kind.' The statements *'after its kind'* and *'whose seed is in itself"* are repeated several times throughout the creation account, underscoring the generational approach with which God set into motion all living beings.

God's first words ever spoken to man were "Be fruitful..." God created Adam, blessed him and then said, "Be fruitful, multiply, replenish the earth and have dominion" (Gen. 1:28). Generational thinking is part of our God-given mandate. It is our responsibility to think generationally and approach our assignment with a generational mindset. Generational thinking is a foundational principle that God has used from the beginning. It is this same generational principle that we must use in fulfilling His plan for us.

Over the years, as my family has traveled back to the United States to visit family and dear partners who faithfully support us, we are often asked if we are fearful. I seem to always get a question about snakes and their impact on my life. The truth is, living in Africa offers many adventures that are outside what my American peers might consider "normal," but I can honestly say that I have never been afraid of those differences. I am not afraid of the snakes. I am not afraid of wearing the "different" clothes – West Africa is known for some of the most beautiful, flowing robes that both men and women of all faiths wear. I am not afraid of eating food that is looking back at me. I am not afraid of using the toilet where there is no toilet.

However, if there is one thing that would give me cause for fear, it would be that the ministry where we have labored for years would not continue; that after having lived our lives in some tough places, hot places, and challenging places, and after having made the sacrifices that missionaries must make, that, after all of that, our fruit would not remain. The idea that our work would have no lasting impact is the only thing that would keep me awake at night.

We have not been appointed to simply bear fruit, but that we would bear fruit that remains. We must all be verifying that our work will have an ongoing effect. For us as missionaries working in different cultures, we must strive to find the right strategies that will ensure sustainability. Every culture is unique and demands a model that is right for each specific people. However different the strategies might be to ensure relevancy, we must *all* have a generational mindset to the actual work.

From the initial stages of our efforts, we should consider the long-term goal. Built into our strategies must be the generational component that ensures sustainability. Our model for fulfilling our assignment, whether it is in missions or in other occupations, must be producing fruit that is sustainable. Fruit that remains. Jesus made it clear that He chose us and appointed us for this purpose. Apparently, it was not enough to simply tell us to bear fruit that remains, but rather show it to be worthy of the Lord's forethought, and appointment. Our mandate of bearing fruit that remains is why generational thinking is required to fulfill our purpose.

There has been a trend among churches in recent years to shift their missions strategies away from long-term missions and into short-term mission trips. There are obvious advantages to short-term trips. By exposing congregations to the mission field, people see, first-hand, the bigger world around them and the huge need for the Good News of Christ. They get a small taste of the adventures of the Great Commission. They are even inspired to invest financially into the missions work. It is also through short-term trips, that a faithful few respond to the call of God on their lives to serve in full-time missions.

Short-term trips can provide a quick return on investment – particularly for the sending church – as there is an immediate spiritual awakening in the lives of those who were sent. However, the actual impact – both from the sending congregation and the receiving field - might be less tangible. Short-term strategies that are not linked to long-term strategies oftentimes deliver short-lived results. We put at risk our mandate to yield *"fruit that remains."*

The "career missionary," committed to a life of full-time ministry in a foreign land, seems to be on the decline. While much of the world is evangelized and churches are raised up and led by indigenous leaders, there remain many places where missionaries – from all nations - are desperately needed. Indeed, there are corners of this world that do not have a witness for Christ and need long-term missionaries with a generational commitment to bring the apostolic foundation.

"You did not choose Me, but I chose you..."

Growing up I struggled to understand what Jesus meant when He said, "You did not choose Me, but I chose you..." Yet, I distinctly remember choosing Jesus. When I realized that I needed forgiveness, I made a decision to invite Jesus into my life. Repentance is a decision. So why is Jesus telling His disciples that they did not choose Him but that He chose them?

While I am aware of various doctrines associated with predestination, I lean toward an Arminian free-will understanding of our salvation. I believe we must accept Jesus as our Lord and

Savior by choosing to repent. We must choose Jesus. Just like Joshua said to the Israelites, "choose you, this day, whom you will serve."

It was during my freshman year at ORU that I came to better understand the meaning of Jesus' words. The dorms at ORU are organized with each men's dorm being matched to a women's dorm by assigning each men's floor (wing) to a corresponding women's floor (wing) to have a brother/sister wing identity. There are various events planned by student leaders including fellowship activities, intramural sports, and eating meals together in the cafeteria that bring these brother/sister wings together. One of the optional activities included brother/sister wing prayer partners. A student from the brother wing could choose to be randomly assigned a prayer partner from the sister wing to share prayer needs and pray together.

I signed up for a sister prayer partner. When the final list of brother/sister prayer partners was posted, I learned that I had been assigned to Danette Goodmanson. By the way, Danette is now my wife, so you can see where this story is going. Shortly after learning that Danette would be my prayer partner, I happened to see her in the cafeteria. I approached her confidently. "Hey," I said. "We're going to be prayer partners." What I did not know is that Danette, who was one year ahead of me and also the chaplain of the sister wing, was actually the person who was responsible for creating the brother/sister prayer partner list. I later found out that when she created the list, she had specifically chosen me as her prayer partner before she continued with the task of drawing names out of a hat for random pairing.

So, you can imagine what she was thinking when I saw her in the cafeteria and said, "Hey, I am going to be your prayer partner." She was thinking, "You did not choose me. I chose *you*."

When we choose Jesus, and we certainly *do* choose Him, He says to us "You didn't choose me, but I chose you." Before the foundations of the world, God had looked across the generations. He saw our choice before the beginning of time and said, "I choose you and appoint you to be fruitful." Our God is the God of Generations. David declares it to the Lord in Psalm 145 "Your Kingdom is an everlasting kingdom, and your dominion endures through all generations."

We have been chosen and appointed to bear fruit that remains. Fruit that remains is generational. Fruit that remains is more than a natural result of being alive, it is an intentional reproducing of the transforming life of God in you.

Fishers of Men

Matthew 28:18-20 - *"And Jesus came and spoke to them, saying, 'All authority has been given to Me in heaven and on earth. Go therefore and **make disciples of all nations**, baptizing them in the name of the Father and of the Son and of the Holy Spirit, teaching them to observe all things that I have commanded you; and lo, I am with you always, even to the end of the age.' Amen."* NKJV

Discipleship is the essential component to every Great Commission strategy. Discipleship is not an optional method to incorporate in spreading the Gospel, it is the principal process exemplified and commanded by our Lord Jesus. We have been charged with the responsibility to make disciples of all nations. Generational thinking is never more clearly demonstrated than in discipleship.

Discipleship is about reproducing yourself in others. Reproducing the transformed life of God in you to others. An "each one, reach one – each one, teach one" model is the essence of discipleship. While it involves teaching, training, discipline, guidance, transformation, and relationship; discipleship is, ultimately, about reproducing. From the calling of the first disciples, Jesus revealed to us the essential component of generational commitment in discipleship.

Matthew 4:19 - *"And he saith unto them, Follow me, and I will make you fishers of men." KJV*

Following Jesus sets us on a course of reaching others. Jesus' plan was not just to have people following Him, but to have people transformed and reproducing. He was not just obtaining followers, he was raising up leaders. Being a disciple is more than just following, it is leading others to follow as we also follow. Paul said it clearly in I Corinthians 11:1 *"Follow my example, as I follow the example of Christ."*

Jesus did not try to preach and disciple everyone himself. Rather, we see that he invested mainly into twelve men with the expectation that those twelve men would carry the Gospel around the world. He demonstrated a generational mindset when he raised his disciples to do the works that he did. He sent them out to minister in His name, heal the sick, cast out demons, and raise the dead. He reproduced Himself in His disciples so that they would, in turn, reach others with the same transforming power of God's Spirit.

Two thousand years after Jesus demonstrated ministry to his disciples, His example continues today. Saidou, a young man trained in our ministry exemplifies what it means to follow the example of Jesus in bringing liberty to those in bondage.

In the middle of the night, Pastor Saidou was awakened by a banging on the zinc door of his mud brick house. As he came out, he could see that many of the people in the village had been up for some time dealing with a problem. He was informed that a young boy had gone crazy and had been screaming and throwing himself about uncontrollably. The malams (local Muslim clergy) had done all they knew to do, with no results. They had reluctantly decided to wake up the Christian in the village, Pastor Saidou, to see if he could help.

The crowds parted as Pastor Saidou, a short fiery young man, made his way to where the boy was being held. The door to the mud hut was unlocked for the pastor to go inside. I can still hear Pastor Saidou's voice as he recounts the experience of meeting the troubled boy, face to face, and commanding the demons to shut up and release the boy. As quickly as Pastor Saidou had gone into the hut, he came out with a transformed young boy. The boy was at peace and in his right mind. He had been completely set free. The example of ministry set forth by Jesus to His disciples continues to this day.

Discipleship is based on generational thinking. Jesus says in John 15:8 that *"by this My Father is glorified, that you bear much fruit; so you will be My disciples."* Fruitfulness is a determining element of being a disciple of Jesus.

2 Timothy 2:2 - *"And the things that you have heard from me among many witnesses, commit these to faithful men who will be able to teach others also." NKJV*

The apostle Paul was generational in his approach to the Great Commission. In his instruction to his son in the Lord, Timothy, he emphasizes the importance of thinking generationally. Four generations are represented in this one verse that he writes in his letter to Timothy. He says, "The things you (**Timothy - #1**) have heard from me (**Paul - # 2**) among many witnesses, commit these to faithful men (**faithful men - #3**) who will teach others (**others - #4**) also." Paul's words to Timothy should compel us today to organize our efforts around a generational model of ministry.

"Evangelism without discipleship is a waste.

It is a waste of time, money and effort."

I have made this statement several times when preaching to fellow believers. Each time I say this, I notice a pause, or silence, rather than any reinforcing "Amen!" It may seem harsh or, perhaps, extreme. But we must remember the charge of our Lord Jesus was that we make *disciples* of all nations, not just converts.

The pressure to share impressive statistics of salvations and healings seem to have pushed many evangelists to report exaggerated numbers. The truth is that it is not about the number of hands raised, but about the lives that have been transformed. The Gospel is the "power of God to salvation for everyone who believes" (Rom. 1:16). However, hearing the Gospel message, and even responding to it, without receiving any follow-up discipleship has caused many new converts to harden their hearts. I believe the neglect of intentional discipleship after evangelism can be worse than never evangelizing at all. Without discipleship, people who may have expressed interest in knowing Christ might easily and permanently reject the Gospel, out of a feeling of abandonment.

We saw this tragedy in villages in Niger where a US Christian organization had been working. This organization had a mandate to evangelize these villages. Their teams were to go from village to village to show a film of Jesus' life after which, they would record the responses to a call for salvation. You can imagine the results were quite positive, even in a predominantly Muslim area. Most of these villages lacked basic amenities like clean water or electricity, and the people had never seen movies.

Unfortunately, the organization only focused on the evangelism with no plans for discipleship, or at least no emphasis on discipleship. Their funding was dependent on the number of times the film was shown, not on any level of discipleship. On multiple occasions, local pastors within our ministry – one with a church-planting focus - would come across villages where many people had seen the film and understood the story of Jesus. And although they had been initially open and excited about what they had learned, they quickly became disillusioned and hardened to the Gospel when there was no follow up. By the time we happened to reach their village, they were feeling abandoned after being vulnerable to respond. They had decided to reject any further outreach to them.

Obviously, evangelism is necessary. The "Jesus Film" has transformed lives of millions of people. I grew up in a church whose motto is, 'Evangelism is Our Supreme Task.' But we must ensure that evangelism is always implemented together with discipleship. Discipleship goes beyond the present moment and requires a generational commitment. Jesus highlights this in John chapter 8 when he makes a distinction between being a believer and being a disciple.

John 8:30-31 – *"As He spake these words, many believed on Him. Then said Jesus to those Jews which believed on Him, 'If ye continue in my word, then are ye My disciples indeed; And ye shall know the truth, and the truth shall make you free.'" KJV*

There is a marked difference between believing His word and continuing in His word. It is the *continuing, abiding,* or *remaining* in His word that distinguishes us as His disciples. It is not just about a momentary response to a presentation of truth, but a life-change response that is brought out through the process of discipleship.

I am not saying that a person is not saved the very moment he cries out to the Lord in faith. "For whosoever shall call upon the name of the Lord shall be saved" (Romans 10:13). However, to fulfill the Great Commission, we must think generationally and focus on making disciples.

Discipleship begins with evangelism. Discipleship goes beyond evangelism. Discipleship is an ongoing process based on relationship between teacher and student. Discipleship involves commitment, change, sacrifice, and even death.

Luke 9:23,24 – *"Then he said to them all, 'Whoever wants to be my disciple must deny themselves and take up their cross daily and follow me. For whoever wants to save their life will lose it, but whoever loses their life for me will save it." NIV*

Luke 14:33 – *"So likewise, whoever of you does not forsake all that he has cannot be My disciple." NKJV*

The specification of taking up your cross daily to be His disciple teaches that discipleship is not just a response to the Gospel message, but it is a process -- an ongoing day-to-day experience of denying yourself and dying to self. As disciples of Christ Jesus, we are called to daily lay down our desires and embrace His plan. We forsake all in order to be counted among His disciples.

Just as Paul teaches in Romans chapter 12 that we are to "present ourselves unto God as living sacrifices," he also instructs us not to "be conformed to this world but be transformed by the renewing of our minds." This is an ongoing transformation that takes place in the lives of those who make the commitment to be His disciples. The renewing of the mind is a continuative tense showing a process of change through continual, consistent teaching. Generational thinking is never more clearly demonstrated than in discipleship.

Chapter Nine

Make Room

Isaiah 54:1-3 - *"'Sing, barren woman, you who never bore a child; burst into song, shout for joy, you who were never in labor; because more are the children of the desolate woman than of her who has a husband,' says the Lord. 'Enlarge the place of your tent, stretch your tent curtains wide, do not hold back; lengthen your cord, strengthen your stakes. For you will spread out to the right and to the left; your descendants will dispossess nations and settle in their cities.'"* NIV

This is a prophetic word for Israel concerning the future glory of Zion. It is impressing upon the people that they need to make room for the next generation. The barrenness of the past is soon to be a distant memory. The Lord has a plan of greatness for Israel's coming generations. He is getting ready to turn the barren and desolate situation of God's people around for His glory.

This wonderful plan for the next generation comes with instruction. He tells them to enlarge their place and to extend the walls of their dwelling. He tells them they need to make room for what is to come. The Lord is stirring up their expectation. He is mobilizing them to prepare. He is compelling them to make the necessary room for the next generation.

Solomon tells us in Psalm 127:3 that our "children are a heritage from the Lord, offspring a reward from him." When the Lord blesses us with children, it comes with responsibility. Whether they are our natural children or our spiritual children, it makes no difference. We have the responsibility to teach, to train and to pass on to them the covenant truths, just as we saw earlier with Abraham's example. We must also recognize our responsibility to make room for the next generation and give them the space to grow in their calling.

We must increase our vision to include the next generation. We must increase our capacity to reach beyond our own mandate. Children should have their place. Children should know their place. They should have the freedom and confidence to make choices, to make mistakes, and even, to fail. Without the opportunity to fail, there is really no opportunity to succeed. The tendency to smother our children is based on fear. Too many parents want to do everything for their children. And the children will let them. But that does not allow the children to take their place. It keeps their world small. We must provide the space for them to grow up and become all that God has called them to be.

We were once embarking on our long trip back to Niger where we had raised our three children while serving as missionaries among the Hausa people. A last-minute purchase of our plane tickets resulted in us not being able to sit together. Fortunately, my wife was just a couple of rows from our fifteen-year old son and was able to overhear his conversation with the passenger seated next to him. He was asked why he, as a young American, was travelling to Niger. Our son answered, "*I* am a missionary," not "my parents are missionaries," not "I live there," nor "I go to school there." No, he took full ownership of who he was. I am blessed that my son's identity is not limited by my place or status in life. The next generation must be empowered to be whom they have been called to be. We must give them the space to establish their own place, overcome their obstacles, and build their traditions without limitations of the previous generation.

Many leaders are not willing to make room for the next generation. They are not willing to empower them. They are not willing to give up the authority, the responsibility, the money, or the respect. We often see pastors holding on to their positions longer than they should. Their time has passed. Their influence has faded. Their leadership has dwindled. Ultimately, the church suffers for it. We must enlarge our tent, remove the limitations, and make room for the next generation, empowering them to become leaders.

This word given by Isaiah was not just an instruction to enlarge, but a stirring of expectation for Israel. The word begins with a declaration of joy. O Barren woman begin to sing and begin to shout. Your barrenness is about to be over. You who has never had a child, get ready. Your children are coming! Lots of them! They are going to take over nations!

Expectation is a powerful force. Expectation, like faith, begins with hope. Hebrews 11:1 teaches us that "faith is the substance of things hoped for." Expectation based on what God has spoken triggers faith. It opens the door for God to be involved. We see this in Acts chapter 3 when Peter and John are entering into the temple at the gate called Beautiful. A lame man is begging for some coins. Peter said to him, "Look at us," of which the man did, as he was expecting to receive something. His expectation was stirred. But that day he received a lot more than the coins he was asking for when Peter pulled him up and said, "In the name of Jesus, walk."

We had the opportunity to host Richard Roberts and the Oral Roberts Evangelistic Association in 2007 for the first mass evangelism campaign in Niger. The team mobilized all the churches and ministries to come together for this monumental evangelistic outreach. Working together with so many ministries with a variety of backgrounds can be challenging. There were different ideas on how things should be done, where money should be spent, and even on what name should be assigned to the campaign.

Fortunately, Bishop Boureima Kimso, the president of AMEEN (the national organization representing the evangelical churches in Niger), was a friend of our family and true man of faith. His influence helped us set up the campaign to be faith focused and not religious. The original suggestion put forth to call the outreach was 'National Evangelization of Niger Campaign.' My Dad was quick to nix that idea pointing out that no Muslim would be drawn into a meeting like that. Knowing the anointing on Richard Roberts ministry, he demanded the campaign be called "Miracle Healing Rally." Expectation had been set.

After months of preparation, the Miracle Healing Rally was finally launched. I was sitting on the platform, minutes away from the first-night opener of the campaign, when some pastors came to speak with me. As the crowd swelled with anticipation, these men informed me that there were concerns and grumblings from many of the pastors from other churches who were also in attendance. They wanted to know why we had put a huge banner across the back of the platform that read, "Expect Your Miracle!" They said that it would be a great shame for all the Christians in Niger if there were no miracles. Sadly, that was the mentality of many of the Christians in Niger at that time.

The first night of the rally was incredible. When Richard Roberts finished preaching, he began to pray for the sick, commanding blind eyes to open, lame to walk, and sickness to get out. I remember in that moment, as we stood in line across the front of the platform with Richard proclaiming healing and deliverance, that there was a weight of expectation in the atmosphere. Perhaps to some it was uncertainty or even fear, but for many it was great expectation.

Then all of the sudden, cries and shouts from all over the field began to erupt. God miraculously healed so many that night that Richard later told me that he had never experienced so many miracles on just the first night of a rally. Through the course of the four nights, there were 3,804 salvation responses with cards filled out and assigned to church pastors across the city for follow up and discipleship.

Expectation is a powerful force that triggers faith. I was later told that a Baptist pastor said that before the rally, the Christians in Niger walked hunched over. But that after the rally, Christians walk with their chest out and head held high. His demonstration said it all.

We must place an expectation on the next generation. As a youth pastor years ago, I quickly learned that young people needed to have an expectation put on them to inspire them to their greatness. We quickly learned the necessity of having a vision for our youth ministry. The vision set the expectation and placed a responsibility on the youth for a common purpose. We must give responsibility to those whom we are raising up. In many cases we must let them rise to the expectation.

Too often, parents take the safe road. They lower their expectations on their children so that they will not be disappointed. Earlier I said we must allow children space to fail, however, this is very different from lowering expectations from the onset. We should not expect our children to mess up. We should not expect our children to do less than their best in school. We should not expect our children to do poorly in sports. When we place healthy expectations upon our children, they will either meet the challenge or will grow through the experience of coming up short. However, when we give in to the safe and easy path of lowered expectations, we hold them back.

My daughter, Tanika, is a walking miracle. In 1992, she was born premature after only 24 weeks gestation. She weighed 1 lbs., 7oz. (652 g). Born four months early, Tanika was tiny, to say the least. She could lay flat on her back and fit on the palm of my hand. My wedding ring could fit around her thigh. Her skull structure was so soft that the nurses had to turn her head periodically so that it wouldn't look like a flat tire. Of course, it was months in the hospital. She spent 54 days on a ventilator. However, Tanika eventually came home. God had answered our prayers.

As she grew older, the only lasting effect of her prematurity was her eyesight. She was legally blind, although you would never know it by how she gets around. Her first years of school in Little Rock, were at the Arkansas School for the Blind. She was told that her condition in both eyes, which included a detached retina, would never improve. She was told that her vision, even corrected with glasses, would never be good enough to drive. But she never stopped praying for her eyes to be healed.

Tanika was in high school in Niger when my wife got a call from one of Tanika's teachers. The teacher, a caring missionary serving in the Christian school, was concerned that when Tanika was praying, she was thanking God that her eyes were healed. She didn't want Tanika to be disillusioned in her faith when her expectation of corrected vision was not met. It was a proud moment for me when I heard it. Tanika's expectation should be an example to us all. At the age of 27, Tanika was able to get her provisionary Oklahoma driver's license. Expectation is a powerful force.

We must make room for the next generation. We must put an expectation on the next generation. And we must prepare the next generation. Leaders need to be intentional about preparing those who have been entrusted to them. The fact that no one may have prepared the way for us, does not mean that we, today's leaders, should not prepare for the coming generation. Preparation comes before the manifestation.

True leadership prepares the way for what is coming. True leaders anticipate what is ahead. We must stop being reactionary and take steps to ensure the next generation's success. A Nigerian preacher said it well, "If you fail to plan, you plan to fail." We are responsible to prepare for the next generation. This is more than simply being an example to them. We must empower them with assignments and responsibilities. It will require an investment of time, training, money, and mentorship. It may include land, buildings, or vehicles. It may involve setting up a platform for your sons and daughters from which they can launch.

Let us give them their space to grow. Let us empower them to lead. Let us demand a higher standard, raising the expectation on them to rise to their full potential. Enlarge the place of your tent.

Chapter Ten

Move from the Mats

Philippians 3:12-14 - *"Not that I have already obtained all this, or have already arrived at my goal, but I press on to take hold of that for which Christ Jesus took hold of me. Brothers and sisters, I do not consider myself yet to have taken hold of it. But one thing I do:* **Forgetting what is behind and straining toward what is ahead, I press on** *toward the goal to win the prize for which God has called me heavenward in Christ Jesus."* NIV

The lesson of *"letting go of what you know to grow into what you don't know,"* is one that I am constantly learning, again and again. It is crucial in generational thinking to not hold on to the past. While we must recognize and draw from those who have gone before us, we must be focused on what is ahead. Taking hold of the future requires letting go of the past.

Moses learned this lesson the hard way.

Numbers 20:7-8 *"The Lord said to Moses, 'Take the staff, and you and your brother Aaron gather the assembly together. Speak to that rock before their eyes and it will pour out its water. You will bring water out of the rock*

for the community so they and their livestock can drink.'"
NIV

Moses was to speak to the rock publicly, in front of the people. Water would come out for the people and their animals to drink. It should be noted that God instructed Moses to *speak* to the rock. Up to this point, Moses had never used his voice as a conduit for miracles. He had always used his shepherd's staff. From his first encounter with God at the burning bush, Moses had used the staff to demonstrate the supernatural power of God.

From the first miracle with the staff turning into a snake, Moses would see God's supernatural power unleashed time and again. It was the staff that Moses stretched to the sky and hail began to rain down on Egypt. It was the out-stretched staff that brought locust to devour the Egyptians' crops. It was the staff stretched over the Red Sea that caused the expanse of water to be parted for the Israelites' safe passage. It was the staff, lifted above Moses' head, that defeated the Amalekites in war. In fact, it was with this same staff that Moses had miraculously brought water out of a rock at Horeb.

Now, God was telling Moses to *speak* to the rock. But Moses, in front of the eyes of the people, was not ready to try something new. He was familiar with using the staff to unleash the power of God. Moses stayed with the familiar and comfortable way of getting things done. Once again, with his staff, Moses hit the rock for water to flow.

It cost him the Promised Land.

Numbers 20:12 *"But the Lord said to Moses and Aaron, 'Because you did not trust in me enough to honor me as holy in the sight of the Israelites, you will not bring this community into the land I give them.'" NIV*

After God had patiently put up with so much from the Israelites, many have wondered where his patience was for Moses. How could He have prohibited Moses from entering the Promised Land? We must realize the importance of looking ahead. We must resist the urge to hold on to what we know and are used to. Generational thinking demands that we learn from what is in the past, and also focus on what is ahead.

When you get stuck in the "comfortable," you can easily miss what God is wanting to do. As new missionaries, we were seeking the Lord for specific direction for our work in Niger when the Lord gave me two words, "Loud Voice." Not quite certain what that might mean, I simply wrote it down in my notes and trusted that God would give me more direction when I needed it.

Not long after arriving to Maradi, Niger and visiting the surrounding villages, I realized that radio ministry would be a powerful tool to communicate the Gospel in any part of the country. It did not matter how impoverished the people were – having no electricity, pulling up water by hand from deep wells, and living in mud huts -- everyone seemed to be carrying a portable radio.

We immediately set out -- all prayed up -- to see if the radio station would allow us to preach the Gospel on the air. Niger's population is more than 95% muslim[1] and we were not sure if we would be received.   Knowing now what I should have realized then was that to be on air was simply an issue of money. Almost immediately, we were on the airwaves sharing the Gospel. The vision that the Lord impressed on me was to have the local Nigerienne pastors, former Muslims, share their testimonies of salvation and preach a Gospel message – one that did not shy away from proclaiming Jesus as the Son of God. Our weekly program was called "Muriyar Ceto" [MU-ree-yar CHE-toh], which, in Hausa, means Voice of Salvation.

Not too long after we began preaching on the radio, I was informed by some of the long-standing and well-established pastors and missionaries, that our program was causing problems for the Christians in the area. There were a couple of issues that seemed to be upsetting the status quo. First, I was told that I should know that you never tell a

Muslim that Jesus is the Son of God. Really? Well, it is true that this truth can be seen as offensive – the idea that God would have a son. Regardless, this concern did not have merit as we were on air with the sole purpose of sharing the Gospel of Christ. Jesus himself said that it was on the revelation that Jesus is the Son of God that He would build His church. We felt this should not be hidden, and so we made it the theme of our messages. Second, we were told that the pastors did not need to be shouting with such a loud voice when they were preaching. Immediately the two words from the Lord, now buried in my notes, came back to me. *Loud Voice.* Confirmation, I knew we were on track.

Apparently, there was already a Christian program broadcasting on another station. That program had been on air for years, but in a very different format that did not seem to bother anyone. We must guard against being entrenched in the familiar and the comfortable. Generational thinking demands that while we draw from those good things that have gone before us, we must take the risk of letting go in order to attain what the Lord has in store for us.

After a couple of years on the radio, our ministry was violently attacked. The attack was directly linked to our radio program. The burning of our church was one of the first of its kind in Niger.

Prior to 2000, when this took place, there had been little or no threat nor reason to come against Christians. Yes, those bold and fearless pastors preaching with *loud voices* did cause some problems for the Christians. Indeed, our ministry facility was directly targeted. But these were necessary problems in which believers were challenged to finally take a stand for the Gospel. The attack on our compound, which included the destruction of both church and Bible school buildings represented a great financial loss, but for the Gospel witness, it was a big win.

After this event, our ministry became known throughout the country as the story was captured on national TV news coverage and international media including Voice of America and BBC radio. Something changed. We started receiving invitations from curious individuals from far-flung villages, requesting that we come and share our message with them. On several occasions, I was recognized at police checkpoints and asked for Gospel tracts, so that they might understand our message.

Generational thinking demands that, while we honor those who have labored before us, we press forward to what is ahead. I remember a discussion about whether the Christians should be sitting on benches or sitting on mats when they gather for fellowship and teaching. One of our newer missionaries was providing benches for the new converts to sit and listen. An older, more experienced missionary happened to be passing by and noticed the benches. He pulled the young new missionary aside to advise him. He let him know that in the Hausa culture, they prefer to sit on mats. As such, there was no need for this young missionary to struggle to get benches. After thanking the older missionary for his advice, the young missionary asked the new converts if *they* preferred mats to the benches. They quickly responded, "Of course not, but benches are much more expensive. That is why we usually use mats. They are cheaper."

Generational thinking looks forward. We must not be limiting the next generation by our own assumptions, preferences, and misunderstandings. The next generation must be free to move from mats to benches. They must be free to reach their full potential. When the next generation is ready, we must yield ourselves so they can move forward. The transition of leadership in an organization is the most authentic demonstration of generational thinking.

In 1998, we moved to Niger for the first time to work with my parents who are known affectionately as "daddy and mummy" by many of our co-laborers in the ministry. My parents, after having spent 15 years serving in Nigeria, which sits on the southern border of Niger, had picked up their tent and moved north to pioneer a church-planting ministry called, *Vie Abondante* (Abundant life).

Many have wondered what it must be like to work directly with your own parents. Fortunately for us, Dad and Mom were intentional in empowering others. Their leadership inspired many to join the team, which has been a hallmark of *Vie Abondante's* growth. Missionaries from Nigeria and from the US came together to strengthen the leaders in Niger being raised up in ministry.

After fifteen years of leading *Vie Abondante*, Dad stepped down and I was installed as the president. Transition of leadership is always a test of the organization's strength and stability. The example of handing off leadership while Dad was still strong and capable to lead set a precedent for *Vie Abondante* that is not common in African cultures. The transition was seamless as I had already been leading in many areas of the ministry.

I served as president for twelve years when the Lord impressed on my heart to release the next generation of leadership. My decision to transition leadership was not because I was tired of leading or even wanting to leave. It was knowing that the next generation was ready. Generational thinking gives a perspective that sees beyond the moment.

In 2018, I handed over the leadership of *Vie Abondante* to one of the Nigerienne pastors who had been raised up in our ministry, Reverend Hashimou Ousmane. He was a son of the ministry who had the heart of a father. He was ready. The ministry was ready. It is said that the goal of a missionary is to work himself out of job. A mature church is self-supporting, self-propagating, and self-governing. Transition to an indigenous leader was significant from a missions strategy perspective, but more importantly to me, it was about being generational.

Reverend Hashimou and I continue to serve together as he leads our ministry to higher levels. I am his biggest supporter. His success is my success.

Chapter Eleven

Not Many Fathers

1 Corinthians 4:15 - *"For though you might have ten thousand instructors in Christ, yet you do not have many fathers; for in Christ Jesus I have begotten you through the Gospel." NKJV*

The Church is blessed today with thousands of teachers in almost every nation and language. There are Bible schools, seminaries, and theological institutions all around the globe. The Lord is using many gifted men and women to teach and equip the body of Christ, giving instruction and passing on their knowledge to others.

The Apostle Paul's distinction between teachers and fathers provides insight into the uniqueness of a father in Christ as opposed to a teacher in Christ. A father does not just teach, but he imparts. A father is part of the reproduction process. A father nurtures, corrects, and provides for his children. Paul is a father to the Corinthians because he was the one God used to bring them into faith through the Gospel. He was not merely a teacher to them but the one who led them to a new life in Christ.

Paul's words teach us a broader scope of fatherhood that extends beyond children born of flesh and blood and includes spiritual children who are raised in the faith. He calls the Corinthians "my beloved sons" and says he has "begotten" – or fathered -- them through the Gospel. He refers to Timothy in many passages as "my son." Titus and Onesimus are also referred to as Paul's sons. These are two men whose salvation story was directly linked to Paul's role of bringing them up in the ways of the Lord. The fatherhood of spiritual sons demonstrates the generational thinking that is at the core of an apostolic work and most definitely core to the discipleship process.

Paul clearly indicates that we may have those in our lives whom we identify as spiritual fathers. By his statement to the Corinthians, we understand that while there may not be many fathers in our life, there can be more than one. God may use various men and women leaders in different seasons of your life to "father" you spiritually as you grow in your walk with the Lord.

Recognizing your spiritual fathers is noble and proper. Proverbs teaches to give honor to whom honor is due. However, it should never be taken to an extreme. We must never allow our honoring of God to be substituted with the honor of men. Unfortunately, I have seen abuses over the years where the spiritual fathers have taken a posture of authority that is reserved for God alone. Pride, manipulation, and control become increasingly evident when the spiritual fathers overstep their boundaries.

We must be vigilant to avoid the extremes. Honor of a man should never be worship. Unfortunately, there are spiritual fathers and ministry leaders who are demanding a culture of respect that goes beyond the honor described in scripture.

Sometimes, this overstep is manifested in very simple things. I have often observed spiritual fathers surrounded by "sons and daughters" whose sole purposes and identities are wrapped up in the promotion or exaltation of their spiritual fathers. Their actions include carrying the leader's Bible and providing very public and over-the-top assistance for him during the service. Of course, these actions can be done tastefully and can certainly exhibit love and honor. But if these actions are mandated to remind everyone that the spiritual father is, indeed, a "big man", then the act of service and honor is quickly lost. Too often, the demands of the fathers for special treatment and ostentatious introductions have ushered in a type of idol worship into our churches.

So much of this is motivated by inflated egos. The grandiose titles that leaders have taken for themselves do not line up with the spirit of servanthood leadership that Jesus taught and demonstrated. While I appreciate a comfortable seat in the service as much as anyone, the thrones that are being erected in churches today seem to draw glory to the man, not to God. They do not send the message of being a father that promotes his sons, but a message of being a king that looks down upon his subjects from on high.

Jesus deals with this in Matthew chapter 23 when He is teaching His disciples to not be like the Scribes and Pharisees who do their works only to be seen by men.

Matthew 23:8-10 *"But you are not to be called 'Rabbi,' for you have one Teacher, and you are all brothers. And do not call anyone on earth 'father,' for you have one Father, and he is in heaven. Nor are you to be called instructors, for you have one instructor, the Messiah."* NIV

Jesus' statements to his disciples are direct as He deals with the pride and arrogance of the Scribes and Pharisees. Most commentaries agree that from the context of this passage, Jesus is not forbidding the use of all titles. He is instructing us not to use any name or title in a way that would usurp the Lord's position of honor, glory, and authority. According to *Gill's Exposition of the Entire Bible*, Jesus *"does not mean to set aside all names and titles...but only to reject all such names and titles, as are used to signify an authoritative power over men's consciences, in matters of faith and obedience."*[1] In other words, we must be careful to not attribute to man, what belongs to God.

Of course, we should appreciate the spiritual fathers in our lives who have been instrumental in our spiritual development. We should also be ready to serve as a spiritual father (parent) to those sons and daughters placed in our lives. However, whether we are the spiritual father or the spiritual child, we should always safeguard against extremes and seek to serve God with a generational mentality and commitment.

Moses was considered by Jewish tradition as the greatest prophet. Most would also agree that Moses was one of the greatest leaders of all time. The massive task of leading the children of Israel out of slavery and through the blazing hot desert for 40 years is probably one of the most difficult feats of leadership in human history. The weight of the leadership was so heavy and the grumblings of the people so difficult that the day came when Moses had finally had enough. He cried out to God in Numbers chapter 11.

Numbers 11:11-15 "...*Why have you brought this trouble on your servant? What have I done to displease you that you put the burden of all these people on me? Did I conceive all these people? Did I give them birth? Why do you tell me to carry them in my arms, as a nurse carries an infant ... I cannot carry all these people by myself; the burden is too heavy for me. If this is how you are going to treat me, please go ahead and kill me...*" NIV

Even as great of a leader as Moses was, he still faced days when everything seemed unbearable. It is in Exodus chapter 18 that we see Moses being mentored by a father. Jethro, Moses' father-in-law, was used by God to give advice to the great leader of Israel. No matter how great of a leader you might already be, allowing a spiritual father to speak into your life will only make you more effective.

Moses was under the strain of leadership responsibility. All of his time and energy was being drained as he provided counsel and solutions to every detailed problem each person brought to him. Jethro visited Moses and it did not take long for Jethro to see that Moses needed some advice. He called Moses over and said, "What you are doing is not good."

Exodus 18:17-19 *"Moses' father-in-law replied, 'what you are doing is not good. You and these people who come to you will only wear yourselves out. The work is too heavy for you; you cannot handle it alone. Listen to me now and I will give you some advice, and God may be with you.'"* NIV

Every leader should have those people in his or her life who can openly say, "what you are doing is not good." Having a Jethro in your life gives you security and stability. A Jethro can point out your mistakes, or even dangers that you do not see. Sadly, many leaders do not want to hear from the Jethros God has placed in their lives. These types of leaders are often afraid to show weakness or be transparent enough to accept the advice of spiritual fathers in their lives.

Jethro serves as a type of mentor to Moses in the area of leadership. By advising Moses to develop a structure of delegated responsibility and authority, he mentors Moses on how to safeguard his energy and health and become a more effective leader. Not only does this counsel make Moses more effective, but it also opens up more leadership opportunities for those Moses has delegated through this new structure.

Mentoring, as a discipline, has been around since the beginning of time, even before it was given its name in Homer's ancient Greek poem, **Odysseus**.

Mentoring is described in Wikipedia as "a relationship in which a more experienced or more knowledgeable person helps to guide a less experienced or less knowledgeable person."[2]

Mentorship is a well-studied and adopted discipline in both faith and secular circles alike. Following is a summarized list from entrepreneur and investor John Rampton showing the advantages of having a mentor in your life:

10 Reasons Why a Mentor is a Must[3]

1. Mentors provide information and knowledge.
2. Mentors can see what you cannot, where you need to improve.
3. Mentors stimulate us to grow and develop.
4. Mentors encourage and keep us going.
5. Mentors can correct us and give boundaries difficult to do ourselves.
6. Mentors can give ear to our ideas without judgement.
7. Mentors are trusted advisors.
8. Mentors can be connectors.
9. Mentors can save you from making mistakes by sharing their experiences.
10. Mentors are free which makes them priceless.

It is invaluable to have a mentor. Mentors will not limit you, but they will increase you. Joshua had a mentor in Moses, and we see Joshua went on to do what his mentor could not. Joshua led the children of Israel into the Promised land and completed the mission Moses had set out to accomplish. Elisha had a mentor and he received a double portion of the anointing of his mentor, Elijah. We can all benefit from mentors at various stages of our lives.

While a spiritual father may fulfill the role of a mentor, not all mentors are spiritual fathers. Spiritual fathers are those who have been significantly involved in some aspect of your spiritual growth and development. There is always a generational component in a spiritual father relationship. As we develop generational thinking in our lives and ministries, we should identify those who have gone before us and honor the fathers who have impacted our lives.

We should also look for those God is entrusting to us, that we may serve as a parenting voice in their lives. As a spiritual father (or mother), we should understand that the Holy Spirit is the teacher, guide, and father for every born-again person. We must understand that being a spiritual father does not give us authority over someone's spirituality, but an influence into their lives. It is an honor to be in this position and we must treat it reverently. May we serve as fathers with revelation of generational thinking and commitment, leading others to be leaders.

Chapter Twelve

Mind the Gap

Malachi 4:6 - *"He will turn the hearts of the parents to their children, and the hearts of the children to their parents; or else I will come and strike the land with total destruction." NIV*

There have always been different ideas, values, preferences, and norms that become prevalent from one generation to the next. We casually refer to this as the generation gap. This gap can be seen in common things like preferences of music, clothing fashions, and hairstyles, but it often goes much deeper to philosophical values, political views, societal norms, and work ethic.

We see that as the generations progress, certain predominant traits emerge, giving a unique identity to each of them. Many studies have identified and analyzed the common attributes between the various generations. While there are no specific cutoffs inherent to identifying generations, certain dates have been used to define the generations "based on major cultural, political, and economic influences."[1] Perhaps you have heard of the *Greatest Generation*, the *Baby Boomers*, *Generation X*, or the *Millennials*. Various studies provide an overview of the strengths and weaknesses between the generations which facilitate better communication, collaboration, and cooperation.

The disconnect of generations seems to have become increasingly pronounced in recent times. What was called a generation gap has become a generation canyon. While there may be advantages in the distance between one generation and another, there is also much that is tragically lost. The scripture in Malachi chapter 4, warns of a total destruction when the hearts of the parents and their children are disconnected. The Bible teaches us the necessity of generational thinking and commitment. We are to follow Abraham's example as described earlier and be faithful to command our children after us.

Many would say that the generation gap gives the distancing needed to foster innovation, fresh ideas, and self-development.[2] By separating from and removing limitations of the past generations, we may broaden our perspective, but we also risk losing our identity. Our traditions can be lost, our heritage can be lost, and, even *who we are* can be lost. Self-development at the expense of self-awareness is not a profitable exchange.

It is commonly agreed that generation gaps are caused by longer life spans, faster changes in society, and the increased mobility that we have in modern times.[3] The rapidly shifting culture influenced by popular trends brings tensions between the old and the new. The generations begin to judge each other from their differing perspectives. This finger-pointing may come from either side. For example, the older generation may see the younger as entitled, disrespectful, and unwilling to follow proven paths. Conversely, the younger generation might view the older as being judgmental, controlling, and smothering of creativity. No matter what the specific issues are, these viewpoints create obvious breakdowns in communication and relationship. Misunderstandings, offenses, and bitterness can easily steal an entire heritage. The disconnect of the generations opens the door for chaos and confusion. Continuity is lost and traditions fall by the wayside.

We must not lose the generational commitment to transfer the "way of the Lord." We must seek to bridge the disconnect by reducing the generation gap. Recognizing the dangers of generational disconnect and the awareness of its consequences to our faith should serve as a warning to us. We must bridge the gap.

My wife and I, along with Tobi, our youngest son, once had an opportunity to visit London for a few days. Making our way to the sights were easier than I would have expected in such a large city. Their subway system, the London Underground or Tube, enables everyone to reach all corners of the city quickly. We were soon confident in how to maneuver the Tube and it did not take long for the iconic phrase, *Mind the Gap*, to be etched in our minds. This warning, constantly repeated on speaker thousands of times each day, alerts travelers to be aware of the space between the platform and the train. Years later, I can still hear the lady's recorded voice, "Mind the gap."

We must be mindful of the gap. Not just the gap that offers risk of falling between the platform and the train, but of the gap that risks disconnect between parents and children – between generations. We must find ways to keep communication flowing. We must strengthen the common bonds that unify us as a family and a nation. We must nurture a mutual respect that enables us to accomplish more together.

Tobi has helped me realize that there are valid factors that influence how you may see something differently. The difference of perspective between a father and a son is not always an issue of being right or wrong, just different. At four-years-old Tobi and his best friend in Niger, Fili, were inseparable. The fact that they were from completely different parts of the world made no difference.

One summer, when we were in the US itinerating to our supporting churches, we received word from Niger that Fili had been in an accident. A car had backed over him. Fili survived the incident, but his abdominal region was severely injured leaving him with the inability to control his bladder. When we arrived back to Niger, Tobi and Fili picked right back up as best friends. Fili was constantly at our house playing.

You can imagine the situation. Fili cannot control his bladder. That means his pants were always wet with urine and the smell excruciating. We would try and help Fili by washing his clothes and having him take showers, but the smell was constant. Tobi would ask if he and Fili could play in his room. Danette would say, "OK but stay on the floor. No getting on the bed." Tobi would ask if Fili could come to church with us. We would make sure that they sat in the 'way back' and still I would be driving with tears coming down my face from the ammonia. The stench was horrendous.

One day I came home from teaching all morning at the Bible School. It had been a long morning and I was tired. As soon as I walked through the door, I knew that Fili was in the house. I called Tobi into the room. I told him, "I can't take it today. I need a break. Fili has to go home. The smell is too much."

I will never forget as Tobi innocently looked up at me and said, "What smell?"

That is the moment I realized that Tobi was seeing Fili from a completely different lens than I was willing to peer through. Tobi saw only his best friend. I saw a smelly, uncomfortable burden that I must bear. I realized that my perspective is not always right. My son was seeing much more clearly than me. Each generation needs to realize that it might not be seeing the situation in its entirety. Years later Tobi and Fili are still friends though they live on different continents. As Fili grew up his body healed and he no longer struggles with incontinence.

Every generation, at some point, needs to know that it is significant. Whether it is the emerging generation finding its purpose or the veterans confident of their past victories, each generation needs the reassurance of having value. Ephesians chapter 6 gives us insight in how to "mind the gap" in dealing with each other.

Ephesian 6:1-3 *"Children, obey your parents in the Lord, for this is right. 'Honor your father and mother' – which* *is the first commandment with promise – 'so that it may go well with you and that you may enjoy long life on the earth.'" NIV*

The younger generation is given clear instructions. Obedience and honor set the stage for cooperation and unity. The scriptures even point out the promise of a good and long life that comes with this commandment. Obedience and honor are not difficult when they are balanced with the empowerment of the children by their parents.

The older generation also has a responsibility.

Ephesians 6:4 *"Fathers, do not exasperate your children; instead, bring them up in the training and instruction of the Lord." NIV*

The older generation must be sensitive to the hearts of their children. They must recognize the children's individual needs so that their parenting does not exasperate the children. In other words, the parents should be mindful to not irritate and frustrate them.

Parents have the responsibility to "bring them up." The training and instruction of the Lord should be done to bring them up, not to hold them down. We need to release the next generation to go higher, do more, and reach further. When we hold them back, we will only frustrate them. We can close the gap. We can bridge the disconnect. Honoring our parents and empowering our children are the keys to bridging the gap.

The Apostle Paul writes to Timothy acknowledging the generational heritage of faith in which Timothy was raised. It is an example to be admired and even celebrated.

2 Timothy 1:5-6 *"I am reminded of your sincere faith, which first lived in your grandmother Lois and in your mother Eunice and, I am persuaded, now lives in you also. For this reason I remind you to fan into flame the gift of God, which is in you through the laying on of my hands."* NIV

Too many families have experienced a disconnect in the generations. I have heard many stories of children backsliding from their faith. Many were even children of pastors and missionaries. My heart cries out for these lost ones. Paul's words of remembrance to Timothy should also remind us that we have a responsibility to fan the flames in our generation. It does not matter how great our spiritual background might be or how numerous the generations of believers who have come before, we have a responsibility for our calling. Every generation must have their encounter with God. Every generation must fan the flames of the gift of God in them.

God is a God of generations. His faithfulness endures to all generations. His plan is from generation to generation.

Acts 2:39 *"The promise is for you and your children and for all who are far off – for all whom the Lord our God will call." NIV*

His promise is for you and your children, even your children who are *far off* -- whether they are far off in terms of generations or far off in faith. Your children may be *far off* but, in faith, we call them back. We call back every child that has been disconnected from parents and their heritage of faith. We call their hearts to be turned back to the parents, in Jesus name! And we speak hope to every parent that is hurt and discouraged. Let the hearts of the parents be turned back to their children!

Chapter Thirteen

Choose Your Legacy

Joshua 24:15 - *"But if serving the Lord seems undesirable to you, **then choose for yourselves this day whom you will serve**, whether the gods your ancestors served beyond the Euphrates, or the gods of the Amorites, in whose land you are living. But as for me and my household, we will serve the Lord."* NIV

The power to choose is a theme that can be seen throughout scripture. From Adam and Eve's choice in the garden to eat of the forbidden fruit to Abraham's choice in obeying God's direction to sacrifice his son, Isaac, it is evident that man has the ability to choose what actions he will take. We can make wrong choices and we can make right choices. It is the choices that we make that affect how we live life today as well as prepare for the future.

While there are in-depth studies on *'determinism'* ranging in perspective from theological to metaphysical, it is God's Word that sheds the light needed to understand our power to choose. When Joshua challenges the Israelite people to choose for themselves whom they will serve, he reminds them of other generations' choices. He points out the previous generation's choices to serve other gods. He points out the gods of the current generation of another people. He then proclaims his own choice, with what has now become an iconic phrase, *"But as for me and my house, we will serve the Lord."*

The Israelites needed to make their choice. There were obviously choices available. We have the power to choose. While there are certainly consequences to sin that the Bible indicates -- in numerous passages – that extend to the third and fourth generations, the Gospel can immediately set us free. When we choose to put our trust in the Lord Jesus, His power can break every generational curse and chain of sin's consequences.[1] Galatians 3:13 tells us that Jesus redeemed us from the curse of the law, having become a curse for us.

Scriptures teach us that our future is based on our choices.

Galatians 6:7,8 *"Do not be deceived: God cannot be mocked. A man reaps what he sows. Whoever sows to please their flesh, from the flesh will reap destruction; whoever sows to please the Spirit, from the Spirit will reap eternal life." NIV*

This verse is addressing more than the growth cycle used by farmers. This fundamental principle can be applied across all areas of life. When we make the correct choices, we will benefit the positive outcomes. What we sow is our choice and based on that choice, we will also reap. We must choose whom we will serve. And like Joshua, our choices will affect our entire households. Our choices today will affect generations that come after us.

"Our heritage does not determine our legacy.

We must choose our legacy."

I have made this statement over the years to emphasize our choice and responsibility to pass on to the next generation something honorable. There is an implied distinction between heritage and legacy. Both words have very similar meanings and are often used interchangeably. However, the following definitions highlight the subtle difference that help qualify the quote above.

Heritage - *something you inherit, something you are born into like money, fame, culture.*[2]

Legacy - *something you leave behind like money, fame, and culture.*[3]

The distinction is the perspective of whether you are passing it on to those coming after you, or if you are receiving it from those who have gone before you. Your choices cannot change what was passed down to you – both good and bad --but what you pass on to others is completely within your power. You get to choose your legacy.

I have an incredible heritage. I was born in the United States and enjoyed my early years as a typical American child. At 11 years old, I had the privilege of moving to Nigeria where I experienced the adventures of missionary life in Africa. My parents introduced me to Jesus at an early age. I grew up not only knowing Jesus as my Savior and Lord, but knowing what it meant to be part of the Great Commission. My parents demonstrated God's love and instilled in me a passion for the Lord. The ministry was led by an apostolic leader, Archbishop Benson Idahosa, who ministered boldly with signs, wonders, and miracles, imprinting on my young heart a passion for God and His work.

The incredible heritage handed to me did not mean that my life would automatically follow a path to be admired. It did not mean that my children, in turn, were guaranteed a similar legacy. I had to choose the legacy that I would leave to them. While I never strayed far from the example laid out for me, I have experienced times of deep soul searching, repentance, and correction. We must all choose the life that we live and, in turn, the legacy that we will leave for the next generation.

Understanding that heritage does not determine legacy is both freeing and inspiring. It gives us the hope that no matter how bad and abusive our heritage might be, our legacy can be different. *Your* legacy can be great. Not everyone can testify of having known the Lord at a young age. Many people have had horrible childhoods and experienced unthinkable abuses. Regardless, your heritage does not determine your legacy. You choose the legacy that you will leave for the next generation.

This will require work, and maybe disappointment, as you intentionally pivot from old thinking to new. But, even in this, Christ is with you, giving you power and encouragement through his Holy Spirit. Do not give up on shaping a positive legacy for the next generation – no matter what age you might be. If we are next generation minded and committed to a generational approach to fulfilling God's purpose in our lives, we will experience the success that God's word promises.

I Kings 2:1-4 *"When the time drew near for David to die, he gave a charge to Solomon his son. I am about to go the way of all the earth, he said. So be strong, act like a man, and observe what the Lord your God requires: walk in obedience to him, and keep his decrees and commands, his laws and regulations, as written in the Law of Moses. Do this so that you may prosper in all you do and wherever you go and the Lord may keep his* *promise to me: 'if your descendants watch how they live, and if they walk faithfully before me with all their heart and soul, you will never fail to have a successor on the throne of Israel.'"* NIV

David passes to his son a legacy of God's plan. God's plan is to prosper His people. God's plan is for our fruit to remain. God's plan includes having a successor. David instructs Solomon to make the right choices, because his choices determine his legacy. The greatest legacy that we can leave behind is that our children know the Lord. The Apostle John said it best, *"I have no greater joy than to hear that my children are walking in the truth"* (3 John 1:4). We must choose our legacy.

Chapter Fourteen

Honor Those Who Have Gone Before

Hebrews 12:1 - *"Therefore, since we are surrounded by such a great cloud of witnesses, let us throw off everything that hinders and the sin that so easily entangles. And let us run with perseverance the race marked out for us." NIV*

We are surrounded by such a great cloud of witnesses. The imagery of this verse indicates that we are being watched and cheered on by those who have gone before us. It is no longer a time to look back, but a time to focus on the race that has been laid out for us. Yet, we run with the confidence that we are not alone.

The author of Hebrews begins the chapter with the word "therefore" which is a reference to what he had written in the preceding chapter. He provided an inspiring overview of mighty men and women of faith. The testimonies of great faith in the face of adversity set the stage for us today. Their sacrifices and courage in living out their faith – in spite of their weaknesses and faults -- provides an energizing example that compels us to let go of our own distractions and run our race.

I have always been inspired by the stories of men and women who made an impact on their generation. Many inspiring accounts have been preserved throughout church history. Men and women throughout the generations who have been instrumental in spreading the Gospel and establishing the Church have always stirred my heart, motivating me to do more for the Kingdom. From the heroes of faith recorded in scriptures to those of the generations following, our lives are impacted by their contributions.

I have been fortunate to have had several heroes in my life; those whose lives have been an example to me personally and have played a significant role in my formative years. I am convinced that it is healthy to recognize and honor those who have been 'fathers' in your life.

Ron and Jerry Childs

The earliest and longest running influence in my life have been my parents. Dad and Mom were not only good parents from a natural standpoint of loving, nurturing, and training, but have been spiritual leaders in my life. From my Mom praying with me to ask Jesus into my heart to Dad's teaching and disciplining, both have been faithful to pass on to me the way of the Lord.

I have always seen them as a packaged deal. They are my parents. They have lived the generational example that I urge in this book. As I shared in an earlier chapter, my parents did not only introduce me to Jesus but to the Great Commission. Their passion for missions and their example of ministry have been a major force in my life. They are not fake news. They're the real deal. They are genuine.

Dad and Mom started their missionary adventures in Nigeria where they served in an apostolic ministry experiencing massive church growth. They were in Nigeria for fifteen years in various roles. Dad served as the director of the **All Nations for Christ Bible Institute International**, as well as the crusade director for the Archbishop Benson Idahosa. Mom was the Executive Assistant to the Archbishop for several years. While serving in these high-profile positions of such a well-known, international ministry, their hearts were stirred for the unreached in Niger. They prayed that God would send laborers and He did. God sent them.

After fifteen years in Nigeria, they moved to Niger where they took over a Bible study group and pioneered the church planting ministry, *Vie Abondante*. Today there are 60 *Vie Abondante* churches, 4 *Vie Abondante* Bible Schools, 2 *Vie Abondante* Primary Schools, and a Well drilling ministry. Their humility and faithfulness to the call has always been an inspiration to me.

Archbishop Benson Idahosa

I will never forget, as an eleven-year-old, standing on the back of a crowded crusade field platform watching Archbishop Benson Idahosa preach to 500,000 people. His boldness and rugged faith were forever imprinted on my heart as I watched him reach down and pull up a young boy by his hand. In front of the crowd of thousands he commanded this crippled boy, whose twisted, bony legs were folded up under him to "in the name of Jesus, walk." The image of that boy walking for the first time in his life, across the stage, has never faded from my memory. The Archbishop's culture of faith and miracles still motivates me today to believe God for the impossible.

There are thousands of ministers across the world today who were impacted by this man's life and ministry. Books have been written. Movies have been made. Archbishop Idahosa, described by many as the Father of Pentecostalism in Nigeria, was a legend.[1] He established a denomination with churches around the globe, an international Bible training center and a fully accredited university that bears his name.

This mighty man of God, who ministered in 143 countries,[2] was not just some celebrity preacher, he was a father. In addition to his 4 natural children that bear the Idahosa name, there are countless others that call him 'Papa.' He was a father to many. I consider him to be the spiritual father that God used to stir in me a culture of faith.

He understood the importance of fathering. He took time with people to raise them up. No matter how busy or sought after he might have been, he had a way of connecting at a personal level. At thirteen years old, I started working in the Archbishop's International Office. He would often encourage me. One day after my Mom told him how much I liked his Agbadas (Nigerian four-piece male attire), he gave me one that he had worn to preach in one of his crusades.

When I graduated from Oral Roberts University, he was on the stage sitting next to Oral Roberts himself. When they called my name to receive my diploma, the Archbishop jumped up and came running to give me a big hug in front of the 10,000 people present. He had a way of making you feel like you were the most important person in the room.

He had promised me when I was a child growing up in his church, that when I married, he would come and preach at my wedding. True to his word, he traveled in from another country arriving minutes before the wedding was to start. My Dad was officiating, but Archbishop was to give the message. He said it would be short, about 15 minutes. He actually preached for an hour and had an altar call for marriages that needed healing.

When my wife was pregnant with our first child, he announced to the church with his hand on Danette's tummy that it was his grandson. Truly he was a father. And needless to say, Archbishop was right. It was a boy.

Twenty years after the Archbishop had passed on to heaven, my family was visiting my childhood hometown, Benin City. We went into a local restaurant and I immediately heard the dynamic voice of the Archbishop. He was preaching on the television. All these years later, his voice is still heard. His legacy continues.

Oral Roberts

Making my way through the crowd of other students returning from the ORU chapel service, I felt someone grab my shoulders from behind. Just as I was about to swing around and demand this person 'knock it off' I heard the husky voice of President Oral Roberts say, "Strong shoulders there, son." As a student at Oral Roberts University, I was majorly impacted by this man. I did not know him personally but his influence in my life during those crucial formative college years made him a voice that affected me deeply.

I honor him today as a father in my life, not based on relationship but on impact. It is said that he "was one of the most recognized preachers worldwide at the height of his fame." From his healing crusades to the building of a first-class Spirit-filled university that bears his name, his ministry demonstrated excellence. When I first walked across the ORU campus, through the prayer gardens and under the Prayer tower, I knew that God had brought me there to cultivate and refine His call in me.

As it is often commented on, President Oral Roberts had a plaque on his desk that said, "Make no small plans here." I learned to think big. I learned the importance of excellence. I learned about leadership. Under the umbrella of his ministry, I was fathered in various areas of my life. The Dean of Men, Scott Smith, instilled in me a passion for leadership. The Summer Missions Director, Bill Shuler, inspired me to have a heart for people. The Great Commission was reaffirmed in me to "go into every person's world, to take His light where it is seen dim and His voice where it is heard small, even to the uttermost bounds of the earth."[3]

Years later I am still connected with this tremendous ministry of Oral Roberts through his son, Richard Roberts. What an honor it was to work with President Richard Roberts for the 2007 Miracle Healing Rally in Niamey. Our ministry in Niger is blessed today to be an extension of Oral Roberts Ministry through Richard and Lindsey's support in building a Christian Primary School in Niamey. Our God is a God of generations. His faithfulness endures to all generations. His plan is from generation to generation.

Jerry Pruett

It was immediately after graduating from ORU that Danette and I, newly married, joined Davison Full Gospel Church. Pastor Pruett had founded this Word of Faith church a few years earlier. We were looking for a church as we had just moved into the area with my new job as a Systems Engineer with EDS (Electronic Data Systems).

God used Pastor Pruett to give me opportunities. While I had ministered in Nigeria and on some missions outreach teams, I had never preached in an American church. Pastor Pruett was instrumental in giving me the practical experience I needed to nurture God's call on my life. Danette and I learned so much during those five years that we served as volunteer youth pastors at Davison Full Gospel Church.

One of the most significant lessons was the power of vision. We took over the youth group that was made up of a few young people who didn't really know each other, attended different schools, and were only there because their parents required it of them. At a **Teen Mania** event for youth pastors, we were deeply impacted by the ministry of Ron Luce, and realized that we needed a vision.

In addition to developing our leadership through youth ministry, Pastor Pruett gave me responsibility in the services. He would have me sit with him on the platform, pray with him before the services, and help direct some of the meetings. Serving as what was commonly referred to as an armorbearer to the pastor, I learned invaluable lessons that have helped me in ministry. I am grateful to Pastor Pruett for entrusting me with ministry responsibilities when I was still very green.

Happy Caldwell

Pastor Caldwell is a pastor's pastor. As a gifted Bible teacher, Pastor Caldwell laid a structured foundation of God's Word in my life. He was the pastor who launched Danette and me into the mission field, teaching us to believe God for finances. At a time when popular culture was against talking about money in church, he taught us the importance of tithing. His line-upon-line and precept-upon-precept approach inspired the structure and stability we needed for our ministry. Setting for us an example of consistency and diligence, he cultivated a work ethic in us that keeps us focused on God's purpose for our lives.

It was under Pastor Caldwell's leadership that Brother Terry Nance directed Agape School of World Evangelism (ASWE) where Danette and I received our Bible training. Pastor Caldwell's fathering in my life was certainly enhanced by his armorbearer, Brother Terry, who shared his life everyday with us in the ASWE missions class. When Pastor Caldwell laid his hands on us, ordaining us as ministers of the Gospel, Brother Terry was there in support as well.

Pastor Caldwell's high expectation and standard of excellence has compelled me to give my best. I treasure the days we had at Agape Church and know that our ministry in Niger reflects the spirit of life imparted into us through Pastor's teachings. Danette and I are products of Pastor's vision to produce life - city, state, nation, and world.

Proverbs 20:7 *"The lovers of God will walk in integrity, and their children are fortunate to have godly parents as their examples."* TPT

I am grateful for these five father figures in my life. It is truly fortunate for me to have had godly parents as examples. Generational thinking is never more evident than when we see spiritual children picking up the baton and running the race that has been marked out for them.

Chapter Fifteen

Continue in the Things You Have Learned

2 Timothy 3:14-15 - *"But you must **continue in the things which you have learned** and been assured of, knowing from who you have learned them, and that from childhood you have known the Holy Scriptures, which are able to make you wise for salvation through faith which is in Christ Jesus." NKJV*

A generational approach to ministry is based on continuing in the things which you have learned. From the examples that have been demonstrated to you, you in turn launch out to reproduce. Implementing a generational approach to ministry is about reproducing the things "you have been assured of" and have "known from the Holy Scriptures" just as Paul wrote to Timothy. There will always be those things that you have also learned *not* to do, but hopefully more things that are admirable and able to be emulated.

We can see generational thinking in our church programs. Many churches have done well to design programs geared toward various age groups from the nursery to children's ministry to youth groups to adult Sunday school classes. While these programs are certainly part of the generational approach to ministry, there is the generational mindset, described in the chapters of this book, that must be cultivated and applied to ensure continued advancement.

Many of the churches that emphasize small groups have understood that generational thinking is developed out of relationship. By fostering an environment that places emphasis on relationships, they are experiencing the growth that comes with generational reproduction. The reproducing qualities inherent to generational thinking enable churches to have fruit that remains.

Discipleship and mentorship are often under emphasized in churches, losing the powerful component of generational growth. We need to bring back these fundamental strategies demonstrated in the early church. Discipleship and mentorship programs should be integrated into each church-planting model to ensure that we are building on a foundation that will make us fit for purpose – fit for the future. In Niger, our church planting is based around our Bible Schools and focuses on two areas: discipleship training and leadership training.

Our experience on the field has taught us the importance -- the necessity -- of thinking generationally. Without the Gospel passing from one generation to the next, the church risks falling short in its effort to obediently fulfill the Great Commission. The ability to work as a team, empower young leaders and delegate responsibility, as well as authority, are all critical disciplines required to realize lasting growth.

We must develop generational thinking in our homes and our churches. From the parenting of our children to the preparation of our missionaries, a generational mindset must become our standard model for life. Next-generation empowerment must not be neglected. Their success is our success.

One of the most profound examples that demonstrates the strength and stability of a generational approach to life and ministry is captured in the church burnings that took place across Niger in 2015. Within a two-day period, dozens of churches were attacked and burned across Niger in response to an incident involving French journalist and satirist Charlie Hebdo, of whose weekly newspaper carried the same name. A respecter of no religions, Hebdo, in 2012, published satirical images of the prophet Mohammed. In Islam, it is forbidden to portray any image of the prophet – even in a positive manner. In January

2015, Hebdo was gunned down by Al-Qaeda militants sparking a chain reaction across the globe to not only denounce terrorism, but support freedom of speech. You might recall "Je suis Charlie" (I am Charlie) placards held by demonstrators in front of media outlets at the time. Niger was not spared from this drama and, with a growing increase in radicalized Islamic followers in Niger, the minority group of Christians seemed an easy target.

Thankfully, destruction of property was their main intent, though at least 10 people did lose their lives. Four of our churches were destroyed and two of our pastors lost all of their possessions because they lived on the church grounds. It was an extremely emotional weekend with reports coming in from pastors around the country of attacks and burnings. The official count captured by the media was 45 churches burned. The reality on the ground was a staggering 72 churches attacked and burned. With the smell of ashes filling the air of Niamey, smoke could be seen rising from all sides of the capital city.

In the midst of the chaos and threat of where I was in Niamey, I received a call that in the city of Maradi, we were also being attacked. Maradi is where our original *Vie Abondante* church is located. In fact, this is the same compound that had been burned earlier based on our radio broadcasts. The Maradi church compound is our largest compound with Bible School buildings and pastors' houses.

One of our missionaries in Maradi had come over to the church compound quickly arriving early enough to assist in evacuating those living on the compound before the crowd could overpower the gate. I was told that when he came to evacuate, only the women and children chose to leave for safety. There were 15 youth on the compound that said they would not leave but would stay with the pastor and hold the gate. With crowds that swelled to over 1,000, the 15 young men remained, holding the gate from inside and keeping out the attackers for what ended up being more than four hours until police arrived in riot gear to assist.

These youth successfully held back the crowd from coming in and destroying the Lord's house. Afterward, they said that they were "*jealous* for the house of God." They risked their lives to hold the gate. While the rioters were thwarted at the gate, stones and bricks were hurled over the wall at the youth and buildings inside, breaking the glass windows. At the end of the siege, when the crowds had dispersed, the young boys gathered up all the stones that had been thrown at them and stacked them into a pile. They said the pile was a monument to attest of God's faithfulness. When I saw the picture of the 15 young boys in front of the pile of stones, I saw a monument of generational thinking. These were our children who had grown up in our churches. They were the ones that we played tug-of-war and water balloon games with every year at Children's Camp. This was the next generation.

May our children always fight the good fight of faith. May our sons and daughters live out the plan of God for their lives as we empower them to go higher, do more, and reach further. God is the God of generations. His faithfulness endures to all generations. His plan continues *Beyond One*.

BEYOND ONE

a generational approach to life & ministry

Section: Discussion & Reflection

Digging Deeper

Discussion Questions by Chapter

I encourage you to dig deeper through discussion and reflection. The questions prepared do not specifically have right or wrong answers. They are designed to generate dialogue that will integrate generational thinking into your daily life.

They may be helpful for small group discussion, Bible Study groups, family devotions, or simply personal reflection.

"We've heard true stories from our fathers about our rich heritage. We will continue to tell our children and not hide from the rising generation the great marvels of our God — his miracles and power that have brought us all this far." TPT

Psalms 78:4

Chapter One

Always Another

Vie Abondante Primary School – 3rd Grade Class

"We cannot be so short-sighted that we only live for today. We must learn to think beyond the day-to-day and consider the seasons. And we must learn to think beyond the seasons and consider the generations. We cannot think inside the bubble of a single generation and expect that we will obtain a witness for the Gospel in every nation."

Always Another

1. How does one's culture affect generations?

2. What did you think about Cima getting married at 15 years old?

3. How many generations of your family are alive today?

4. How many generations of your family have you personally known?

5. What are some examples of the best is yet to come? In the Bible? In your life?

6. What are some examples of things getting better with God?

7. How can we keep a generational focus for the Great Commission?

Chapter Two

Tell Your Story

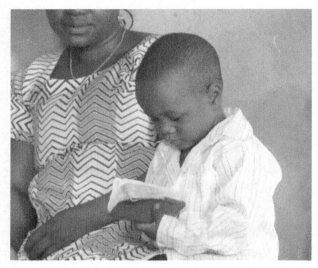

A Mom teaching her son the importance of God's Word

"One of my greatest joys has been to tell my children about my childhood. To share with them the incredible adventures that I had growing up in Nigeria has always been at the top of my 'parenthood' list...It was a responsibility and a privilege to share these stories with my children that I might steer them in a direction that I had been assured of through my own experiences."

Tell Your Story

1. What are the defining moments in your life that you would want to make sure you told your children?

2. What "Red Sea-splitting" kind of miracles have happened in your life that must be told to the coming generation?

3. Are there areas that need renovations in your family? Is the Word getting lost in the busyness of life? What are some strategies not to let that happen?

4. How can we ensure that our story is told?

5. What are some traditions that have helped tell your story?

6. What things have you experienced that you made sure or will make sure that you tell your children?

Chapter Three

Think Beyond One

**Vie Abondante Children's Camp – 460 Children and Captains
An annual discipleship to the next generation.**

"Generational thinking goes beyond one generation.
Thinking beyond one generation not only requires a
generous measure of preparation, it requires an
intentional pursuit."

Think Beyond One

1. What are some things you are preparing for your children?

2. Have you received an inheritance of some kind? What did this inheritance tell you about the person who had passed it on to you?

3. How have you passed on or how would you like to pass on your legacy to your children – natural and spiritual?

4. Recount a time you have reaped where you have not sown.

5. What are some things that have been a blessing to you that were from a previous generation? Like electricity, translated Bible, and telephones, which were already mentioned?

6. What are some of your favorite mission 'one-liner' quotes?

Chapter Four

Next Generation Mentality

The Precious Children are the *Seed* of the Nation

"As Christians, success should be much more than a pursuit of money, fame, power and influence. Success should be based on fulfilling God's purpose. Success should be measured by what God has created us for and called us to do. Living out God's unique plan and calling upon our lives as individuals is the only achievement worthy to be used for identifying success."

Next Generation Mentality

1. What are ways we can think beyond one generation?

2. How did Abraham demonstrate his generational mindset?

3. What do you think about the statement "success without a successor is failure"?

4. How would you describe true success?

5. What does generational commitment look like to you?

6. Besides Abraham, who else in the Bible showed a next-generation mentality?

Chapter Five

Empower to Higher Levels

Niamey Evening Bible School honors our amazing Habibou

"Leaders who do not or cannot take joy in the success of their people should not be in leadership. Leaders should be intentional in seeing their people excel...Leaders should not strive to make followers. Leadership is not about demanding submissive followers to do only what they are told. Leadership is about raising up and empowering others to lead. Leaders produce leaders. The foundational revelation of generational thinking should inspire us to see that our children's successes are our successes."

Empower to Higher Levels

1. What do you think are the greater works that Jesus refers to in John 14:12?

2. In what ways would you want your children to surpass you?

3. What is your reaction when spiritual leaders seem uninterested in empowering their people?

4. Give an example of a leader you have seen help empower others to go higher?

5. Considering this chapter of empowering the next generation, what does Jesus' statement "a student is not above the teacher" mean to you?

6. What do you think about Jesus rebuking his disciples right before entrusting them with the Great Commission?

Chapter Six

Never Abandon

Jesus loves all the children of the world

"We must not abandon our children. We must never neglect to cry out for our children's salvation, protection, and blessing. No matter how bad the situation our children may be in, we can cry out to God. Prayer works. Prayer changes situations.

May our children go higher than we have gone…We pray today for the next generation. We cry out for the purposes of God to be fulfilled in their lives. The Calling of God on their lives will come to pass in Jesus name!"

Never Abandon

1. Have you prayed with all your heart like Hezekiah did to the point of weeping bitterly? Was it for yourself? Was it for someone else?

2. Can you share a time where you feel your prayers turned a situation around?

3. What do you think you would do if you found out something horrible was going to happen to your children?

4. Why do you think Hezekiah did not react to the bad news to befall his family with the same passion as he did regarding his own sickness?

5. Have you cried out before the Lord for yourself? Your children? Others?

6. Do you use a lot of first-person pronouns when you are speaking? What observations can you make about your figure of speech?

7. What do you look for in your life to know if you are caught up in a selfish mentality?

Chapter Seven

Fruit That Remains

**Teekay, a Fulani believer
from our church plant in Diffa, Niger**

"We have not been appointed to simply bear fruit, but
that we would bear fruit that remains. We must all be
verifying that our work will have an ongoing effect. For
us as missionaries working in different cultures, we must
strive to find the right strategies that will ensure
sustainability. Every culture is unique and demands a
model that is right for each specific people. However
different the strategies might be to ensure relevancy, we
must *all* have a generational mindset to the actual work."

Fruit That Remains

1. What are some examples of fruit that we have been appointed to bear?

2. What does it mean that "Jesus appointed us"?

3. How do we ensure that our fruit remains?

4. Did you choose Jesus? Or did Jesus choose you?

5. What do you think about God knowing the end from the beginning?

6. What do the phrases 'after its kind' and 'whose seed is in itself' teach us about God's plan for creation?

7. How do God's first words to man still apply to us today?

Chapter Eight

Fishers of Men

Vie Abondante's first baptism among the Gourmantche

"Discipleship is the essential component to every Great Commission strategy. Discipleship is not an optional method to incorporate in spreading the Gospel, it is the principal process exemplified and commanded by our Lord Jesus."

Fishers of Men

1. Why is discipleship important?

2. How is discipleship generational?

3. What is the difference between being saved and being a disciple?

4. What are some things that identify you as a disciple?

5. What are the four generations in 2 Timothy 2:2?

6. What do you think about the statement "evangelism without discipleship is a waste?"

7. What does it mean to take up your cross daily?

8. How is discipleship a process?

Chapter Nine

Make Room

**Miracle Healing Rally
with Dr. Richard Roberts – 2007 Niamey**

"We must make room for the next generation. We must put an expectation on the next generation. And we must prepare the next generation. Leaders need to be intentional about preparing those who have been entrusted to them. The fact that no one may have prepared the way for us, does not mean that we, today's leaders, should not prepare for the coming generation. Preparation comes before the manifestation."

Make Room

1. How can we make room for the next generation?

2. Why is expectation important?

3. Have you been motivated by expectations?

4. Have you ever been hurt by someone's unreasonable expectations on you?

5. Have you prepared for the next generation? What are ways that you can prepare for the next generation / our children?

6. Have you seen leaders or pastors who do not want to make room? How do you recommend handling that situation?

Chapter Ten

Move from the Mats

Continual Training Programs for Pastors

"Generational thinking looks forward. We must not be limiting the next generation by our own assumptions, preferences, and misunderstandings. The next generation must be free to move from mats to benches. They must be free to reach their full potential. When the next generation is ready, we must yield ourselves so they can move forward. The transition of leadership in an organization is the most authentic demonstration of generational thinking."

Move from the Mats

1. Have you ever felt limited by your predecessors? How should we handle breaking free to do things differently than the previous generation?

2. Have you ever upset the status quo?

3. Are there areas of your life where you are, perhaps, too comfortable and are not willing to change?   Are there habits that God wants you to let go of?

4. Are there things that you can't let go of that keep you back?   Are there things that you need to forget to be able to move on?

5. Have you ever transitioned out of a position to hand over to another? Were you bothered by changes the new leader made?

Chapter Eleven

Not Many Fathers

Vie Abondante Ordination of Rev. Zabeyrou Abdou

"Every leader should have those people in his or her life who can openly say, "what you are doing is not good." Having a Jethro in your life gives you security and stability. A Jethro can point out your mistakes, or even dangers that you do not see. Sadly, many leaders do not want to hear from the Jethros God has placed in their lives."

Not Many Fathers

1. Who are the spiritual fathers (men and women) in your life?

2. Like Moses, have you ever felt overwhelmed by leadership responsibilities?

3. Who are your spiritual children? Who are you influencing?

4. Have you been mentored? What are some examples of how someone has mentored you?

5. Have you ever been a mentor? What did you learn from the experience?

6. What are some of the abuses that you have seen from spiritual fathers?

7. How would you handle an authoritarian father figure in your life?

Chapter Twelve

Mind the Gap

"Let the little children come to Me" - Jesus

"We must be mindful of the gap. Not just the gap that offers risk of falling between the platform and the train, but of the gap that risks disconnect between parents and children – between generations. We must find ways to keep communication flowing. We must strengthen the common bonds that unify us as a family and a nation. We must nurture a mutual respect that enables us to accomplish more together."

Mind the Gap

1. What are generation gap issues you have experienced in your family?

2. What ages were you when you felt a gap?

3. Are there positives from the generation gaps?

4. How do you see self-development versus self-awareness?

5. Have you seen families that have a disconnect between the parents and children? Are there things that you have learned from those examples?

6. What are some practical activities that you can do with children to bridge the gap?

7. Are there instances where you have had a completely different perspective from someone of a different generation than you?

Chapter Thirteen

Choose Your Legacy

Niamey Evening Bible School 2020 - Graduation Joy

"The power to choose is a theme that can be seen throughout scripture. From Adam and Eve's choice in the garden to eat of the forbidden fruit to Abraham's choice in obeying God's direction to sacrifice his son, Isaac, it is evident that man has the ability to choose what actions he will take. We can make wrong choices and we can make right choices. It is the choices that we make that affect how we live life today as well as prepare for the future."

Choose Your Legacy

1. What does the Bible mean about God punishing the children for the sin of the parents to the third and fourth generation?

2. What does the Bible mean about God showing love to a thousand generations?

3. What are some positives that have been passed on in families?

4. What are some negatives that have been passed on in families?

5. How would you describe your heritage?

6. What do you want your legacy to be?

7. Like Joshua, have you chosen a legacy for your entire household?

Chapter Fourteen

Honor Those Who Have
Gone Before

**Transition of Leadership
Installing Rev. Hashimou Ousmane
as President of Vie Abondante - 2018**

"I have always been inspired by the stories of men and women who made an impact on their generation. Many inspiring accounts have been preserved throughout church history. Men and women throughout the generations who have been instrumental in spreading the Gospel and establishing the Church have always stirred my heart, motivating me to do more for the Kingdom. From the heroes of faith recorded in scriptures to those of the generations following, our lives are impacted by their contributions."

Honor Those Who Have Gone Before

1. Who are the heroes in your life?

2. Who are heroes from previous generations you never knew, yet whose lives still impact you?

3. What do you want people to remember about you?

4. Have you ever let those people in your life who have impacted you positively know how much they meant to you? How did they respond?

Chapter Fifteen

Continue in the Things
You Have Learned

Niamey Evening Bible School Graduation 2020

...in all the world as a witness unto all nations...

"Discipleship and mentorship are often under emphasized in churches, losing the powerful component of generational growth. We need to bring back these fundamental strategies demonstrated in the early church. Discipleship and mentorship programs should be integrated into each church-planting model to ensure that we are building on a foundation that will make us fit for purpose – fit for the future."

Continue in the Things
You Have Learned

1. What are some specific, positive things that you learned from someone else that you have now adopted?

2. What are some of the generational approaches that are being implemented in your church?

3. Have you ever been involved in discipleship as either the *discipler* or the *discipled*?

4. Are you part of a small group? Do you invest in relationships with those who will sharpen you?

5. Why is generational thinking so important to the Great Commission?

Scripture References

Introduction

- ➢ Mark 16:15 *KJV*
- ➢ Genesis 15 *chapter*
- ➢ Daniel 4:3 *NKJV*

Chapter 1 - Always Another

- ➢ Judges 2:10 *KJV*
- ➢ Genesis 8:22 *NKJV*
- ➢ Psalms 127:4 *NKJV*
- ➢ Genesis 17 *chapter*
- ➢ Isaiah 43:18,19 *ESV*

Chapter 2 – Tell Your Story

- ➢ Judges 2:10 *KJV*
- ➢ Joshua 4 *chapter*
- ➢ Psalms 78:4 *TPT*
- ➢ 2 Chronicles 34:21 *NIV*

Chapter 3 – Think Beyond One

- ➢ Proverbs 13:22 *NKJV*
- ➢ John 34:37-38 *NIV*

Chapter 4 - Next Generation Mentality

- ➢ Genesis 18:17-19 *KJV*
- ➢ Genesis 12:3 *KJV*
- ➢ Philippians 1:6 *NIV*
- ➢ Deuteronomy 6:5 *NIV*
- ➢ Deuteronomy 6:7 *NIV*
- ➢ 1 Timothy 3:4 *NKJV*

Chapter 5 - Empower to Higher Levels

- ➤ John 14:12 *NKJV*
- ➤ Matthew 10:24-25 *NIV*
- ➤ Mark 16 *chapter*

Chapter 6 – Never Abandon

- ➤ 2 Kings 20:1-3 *NKJV*
- ➤ 2 Kings 20:16-18 *NKJV*
- ➤ 2 Kings 20:19 *KJV*
- ➤ Luke 12:16-21 *NIV*
- ➤ Matthew 12:34 *KJV*
- ➤ John 13:35 *NKJV*
- ➤ 1 Corinthians 13:5 *NKJV*
- ➤ Luke 9:23 *KJV*
- ➤ Romans 12:1 *KJV*

Chapter 7 – Fruit That Remains

- ➤ John 15:16 *NKJV*
- ➤ Genesis 1:28 *KJV*
- ➤ Joshua 24:15 *KJV*

Chapter 8 – Fishers of Men

- ➤ Matthew 28:18-20 *NKJV*
- ➤ Matthew 4:19 *KJV*
- ➤ 1 Corinthians 11:1 *NIV*
- ➤ John 15:8 *NKJV*
- ➤ 2 Timothy 2:2 *NKJV*
- ➤ John 8:33 *KJV*
- ➤ Romans 10:13 *NKJV*
- ➤ Luke 9:23 *NIV*
- ➤ Luke 14:33 *NKJV*
- ➤ Romans 12:1 *KJV*

Chapter 9 – Make Room

- Isaiah 54:1-3 *NIV*
- Psalms 127:3 *NIV*
- Hebrews 11:1 *KJV*
- Acts 3:4-6 *KJV*

Chapter 10 – Press Forward

- Philippians 3:12-14 *NIV*
- Numbers 20:7-8 *NKJV*
- Numbers 20:12 *NKJV*

Chapter 11 – Not Many Fathers

- 1 Corinthians 4:15 *NKJV*
- Proverbs 3:27 *KJV*
- Matthew 23:8-10 *NIV*
- Numbers 11:11-15 *NIV*
- Exodus 18:17-19 *NIV*

Chapter 12 – Mind the Gap

- Malachi 4:6 *NIV*
- Ephesian 6:1-3 *NIV*
- Ephesian 6:4 *NIV*
- 2 Timothy 1:5 *NIV*
- Acts 2:39 *NIV*

Chapter 13 – Choose Your Legacy

- Joshua 24:15 *NIV*
- Galatians 3:13 *NKJV*
- Galatians 6:7-8 *NIV*
- 1 Kings 2:1-4 *NIV*
- 3 John 1:4 *NIV*

Chapter 14 – Honor Those Who Have Gone Before

- ➢ Hebrews 12:1 *NIV*
- ➢ Proverbs 20:7 *TPT*

Chapter 15 – Continue in the Things You Have Learned

- ➢ 2 Timothy 3:14-15 *NKJV*

Section: Discussion and Reflection

- ➢ Psalms 78:4 *TPT*

Notes

1. Wikipedia contributors. "Generation." *Wikipedia, The Free Encyclopedia. Wikipedia,* The Free Encyclopedia, 5 May 2020. 7 May 2020. https://en.wikipedia.org/w/index.php?title=Generati on&oldid=955037124

2. ibid.

3. Coombs, Dean. "What is a Generation in the Bible?" *Bible Code Pictograms,* Dean Coombs, 29 April 2020. https://www.bible-codes.org/old-prophecy_5c-Yeshua-codes

Chapter 1 – Always Another

1. "Niger – What's the Child Marriage Rate." GirlsNotBrides. Girls Not Brides: The Global Partnership to End Child Marriage. 12 May 2020. https://www.girlsnotbrides.org/child-marriage/niger/

Chapter 2 – Tell Your Story

1. "Ronald Reagan Quotes." BrainyQuote.com. BrainyMedia Inc, 2020. 7 May 2020. https://www.brainyquote.com/quotes/Ronald_reag an_183965

Chapter 3 – Think Beyond One

1. Oswald Smith. "Oswald Smith Quotes," goodreads, 2020 Goodreads, Inc. 19 May 2020. https://www.goodreads.com/author/quotes/403672.Oswald_J_Smith

2. ibid.

3. William Carey. "William Carey Quotes," goodreads, 2020 Goodreads, Inc. 19 May 2020. https://www.goodreads.com/quotes/805706-to-know-the-will-of-god-we-need-an-open

4. Mike Stachura. "Mike Stachura Quotes," goodreads, 2020 Goodreads, Inc. 19 May 2020. https://www.goodreads.com/quotes/805701-the-mark-of-a-great-church-is-not-its-seating

5. David Livingstone. "David Livingstone Quotes," goodreads, 2020 Goodreads, Inc. 19 May 2020. https://www.goodreads.com/quotes/805513-christ-alone-can-save-the-world-but-christ-cannot-save

6. David Livingstone. "David Livingstone Quotes," goodreads, 2020 Goodreads, Inc. 19 May 2020. https://www.goodreads.com/quotes/805681-this-generation-can-only-reach-this-generation

7. Barnstone, Willis. "The Bloody History of Bible Translators." Los Angeles Review of Books, LARB Classics, 11 November 2017. https://lareviewofbooks.org/article/the-bloody-history-of-the-bible-translators/

Chapter 4 – Next Generation Mentality

1. Mohla, Neeta. "Success without a Successor is Failure." *C-Suite*, people matters, 4 November 2009. https://www.peoplematters.in/article/training-development/success-without-a-failure-183

Chapter 10 – Move from the Mats

1. "The most heavily Muslim countries on Earth." *CBSNews.com*. 2020 CBS Interactive Inc. 12 May 2020. https://www.cbsnews.com/pictures/most-heavily-muslim-countries-on-earth/16/

Chapter 11 – Not Many Fathers

1. Gill, John. "Matthew 23:9," *Gill's Exposition of the Entire Bible*, Bible Hub, 2020. 7 May 2020. https://biblehub.com/commentaries/matthew/23-9.htm

2. Wikipedia contributors. "Mentorship." *Wikipedia, The Free Encyclopedia. Wikipedia,* The Free Encyclopedia, 31 March 2020. Web. 7 May 2020. https://en.wikipedia.org/w/index.php?title=Mentorship&oldid=948379748

3. Rampton, John. "10 Reasons Why a Mentor Is a Must," *Inc.*, Inc.5000, 9 January 2016. https://www.inc.co/john-rampton/10-reasons-why-a-mentor-is-a-must.html

Chapter 12 – Mind the Gap

1. Robinson, Michael T. "The Generations - Which Generation are You?" *CareerPlanner.com,* CAREERPLANNER.COM Inc, 1997-2020. Web. 7 May 2020. https://www.careerplanner.com/Career-Articles/Generations.cfm

2. Stanleigh, Michael. "The Impact of Generational Differences on Innovation," Business Improvement Architects. 16 June 2006. https://bia.ca/the-impact-of-generational-differences-on-innovation/

3. Williams, Yolanda. "Generation Gap: Definition, Causes & Effects, Chapter 9 /Lesson 10 Transcript." Study.com, 2020. Web. 7 May 2020. https://study.com/academy/lesson/generation-gap-definition-causes-effects.html

Chapter 13 – Choose Your Legacy

1. Milton, Dr. Michael A. "What Are the 'Sins of the Father"? Understanding Generational Consequences." *Crosswalk.com,* Crosswalk.com, 13 February 2020. Web. 7 May 2020. https://www.crosswalk.com/faith/bible-study/what-does-the-sins-of-the-father-mean-in-the-bible.html

2. "Lunarmara." *HiNative.* 2020Lang-8, Inc.   20 Oct 2015. https://hinative.com/en-US/questions/203844

3. ibid.

Chapter 14 – Honor Those Who Have Gone Before

1. Olofinjan, Israel O. "Benson Andrew Idahosa (1938-1998): Father of Nigerian Pentecostalism." *Israelolofoinjana,* 20 Pentecostal Pioneers in Nigeria, 12 March 2012. Web. 7 May 2020. https://israelolofinjana.wordpress.com/2012/03/12/benson-idahosa-1938-1998-father -of-nigerian-pentecostalism/.

2. Agbo, Catherine Forson. "Remembering A Legend: Archbishop Andrew Benson Idahosa (1938-1998)," *Personality Profiles*, Modern Ghana, 31 January 2019. https://www.modernghana.com/lifestyle/13398/remembering-a-legend-archbishop-andrew-benson/hmtl

3. "Vision and Mission." *Oral Roberts University,* ORU, Web. 7 May 2020. https://oru.edu/about-oru/vision-mission.php

REACHING UNREACHED NATIONS

Reaching Unreached Nations International (RUN) was established by Neal & Danette Childs in 2012 to facilitate their vision to reach the unreached. They have been serving in Niger Republic since 1998.

RUN International partners with Vie Abondante in Niger:

Planting Churches

There are currently 60 church plants across Niger, all pastored by nationals that have been trained in Vie Abondante. The goal of our ministry is for every church to be self-supporting and have their own land and building. Church plants typically begin in a thatch structure until the congregation is established and funds are available to build a more permanent building.

Our church planting model not only includes evangelism and discipleship but the purchase of land and buildings as well as strategies to help the pastor become self-supported. This includes farmland for pastors, help to start small businesses and teaching the congregation the principles of tithing.

Bible Schools

Vie Abondante is making disciples and training leaders through structured Bible School settings. The Bible Schools focus on Discipleship and Pastoral training and are available in various languages based on their locations in Maradi, Niamey, and Tamou. The Bible Schools are the backbone for the ministry as it facilitates growth through the evangelism, discipleship, and pastoral training necessary for church planting.

Children and Youth

In the same way your Father in heaven is not willing that any of these little ones should be lost (Matthew 18:14). It is our responsibility as Christians to take the Gospel to the next generation. With 50% of Niger's population under the age of 15, this command is even that much more urgent. The children are the seed of the nation and by reaching them, we reach the nation.

Here are some of the things we do to reach and disciple children.

- Annual Children's Camps for over 500 kids
- Weekly Sunday School in all of our churches
- Writing/developing Children's Curriculum and translating it to the various language groups: Hausa, French, Zarma, Gourmantche
- Training children's ministry workers
- Sunday School Competitions

Primary Schools

Together, we have begun to reach the next generation through Education. Vie Abondante has two Christian Primary Schools starting with pre-school through grade 6.

Over 95% of the children coming to our Christian schools are Muslim. Parents recognize the good education being provided, and are willing to send their children to us, even though their children come home singing about Jesus. This has proven to be a powerful ministry and has opened the door to develop relationships with many Muslim families.

On average the school life expectancy of a child is 5 years. This means that the booming population (50% of the nation's population is under 15 years old) on average have a 5th grade education at best. While education is considered important, opportunities for schooling are sparse. In a nation where only 1 in 3 children attend school, more schools are needed. We have seized this opportunity and have over 700 students in our 2 primary schools.

Children's Homes

There are two children's homes in Vie Abondante to support children through discipleship. Abraham's Place, started and directed by Pastor Koyejo and Lola Amori, serves the Maradi region. Joseph's Place, started and directed by Yolanda Zimmerman, serves the Niamey region. These homes provide a family environment for the children and focus on personal discipleship, education, life skills training and development of individual talent. They are equipping children who are brimming with potential to become leaders and godly influencers in their nation by training them to keep the way of the Lord, to serve, and to live with integrity.

Outreach through development work.

- Vie Abondante with its US based partners Wells 4 Wellness, Faith City Church, and Relief Network Ministries provides bore holes and water pumps for communities in great need.
- Vie Abondante has also helped with food distribution to the most vulnerable during the numerous famine periods Niger has faced in the last 20 years.
- Vie Abondante has been involved in adult Literacy training from its beginning. Using their network of churches, Vie Abondante has successfully taught hundreds to read and write. In a nation with less than 30% literate, it quickly became a priority so that the new believers could read the Bible.

To see what God has done through RUN International's ministry partner in Niger, Vie Abondante, you can purchase the book **'Vie Abondante: The Vision Speaks'** on *Amazon*. The book can serve as a guide to pray for Vie Abondante's churches and ministries.

International Ministry

In addition to their work in Niger, Neal & Danette travel internationally teaching in Bible schools, leadership conferences and women's meetings. Drawing from their years on the mission field, they train pastors and church leaders to inspire more laborers to fulfill the Great Commission.

A Missionary Heritage

Neal grew up as a missionary kid in Nigeria where he saw mass evangelism and mighty miracles on a regular basis. It was there as a young boy that his heart was stirred to take the Gospel where it had not yet been heard.

Danette, raised by Christian parents in Minnesota, had the seed of missions deep in her heart as a child. From the time they met at Oral Roberts University, they have kept a focused commitment to reaching the unreached.

Neal's parents, Ron & Jerry Childs, moved with their children to Nigeria in 1977. From their beginnings in the remote village of Emu where there was no electricity or running water, to their days as the director of All Nations for Christ Bible Institute International, they touched many lives and trained many pastors. They worked alongside Archbishop Benson Idahosa for 15 years before launching out to Niger in 1992. With a pioneer vision of raising up an indigenous church, Ron and Jerry founded Vie Abondante.

Neal and Danette met at Oral Roberts University where Neal graduated with a degree in Management Information Systems and Danette graduated with a degree in Social Work. They were married in 1989 and began working in their respective fields while at the same time were youth pastors in their church in Michigan. While in Michigan, they had 2 children – Trae (1991) and Tanika (1992).

In 1994 they moved to Arkansas to attend Agape School of World Evangelism. From 1994 – 1998 they were part of Agape Church with Pastor Happy Caldwell and continued to work while attending Bible School.

After graduating in 1997, they were appointed as missionaries and immediately went on a 3-week scouting trip to Niger where Neal's parents had moved from Nigeria to Niger to start the ministry of Vie Abondante (Abundant Life). The trip confirmed in their hearts that this was the field they were to serve in and after raising support they moved their family to Niger in July 1998. Their 3rd child Tobi joined the family in March 2000.

Neal & Danette's son Trae graduated from Oral Roberts University in 2013 with a degree in International Community Development. He married Christi Dunagan on June 16th, 2012. Christi, also a graduate of ORU, is from a missions minded family and her parents are founders of Harvest Ministry.

Trae & Christi live and work in the Tacoma, Washington area where they are raising our four beautiful grandchildren, Judah, Charlie Desmond & Oliver.

Tanika graduated from Oral Roberts University in 2015 with a degree in Elementary and Special Education. She is a special-ed teacher in Tulsa, OK. Tanika married Stephen Ezenwosu on July 13th, 2018. Levi was born on August 7, 2019.

Tobi, having lived his life in Niger, is currently a student at Oral Roberts University in Tulsa, OK.

For more about *Reaching Unreached Nations International*: runintl.org

Made in the USA
Monee, IL
09 June 2020